HARV BUSINESS SCHOOL
CONFIDENTIAL
SECRETS OF SUCCESS

Emily Chan

WILEY

John Wiley & Sons (Asia) Pte. Ltd.

Copyright © 2009 John Wiley & Sons (Asia) Pte. Ltd.

Published in 2009 by John Wiley & Sons (Asia) Pte. Ltd.

2 Clementi Loop, #02-01, Singapore 129809

Other Wiley Editorial Offices

John Wiley & Sons, Inc., 111 River Street, Hoboken, NJ 07030, USA

John Wiley & Sons, Ltd., The Atrium, Southern Gate, Chichester,
    West Sussex P019 8SQ, UK

John Wiley & Sons (Canada), Ltd., 5353 Dundas Street West, Suite 400,
    Toronto, Ontario M9B 6H8, Canada

JohnWiley & Sons Australia Ltd., 42 McDougall Street, Milton, Queensland
    4064, Australia

Wiley-VCH, Boschstrasse 12, D-69469 Weinheim, Germany

Library of Congress Cataloging-in-Publication Data

ISBN: 9780-470-822395

Typeset in 10/13pt JansonText-Roman by Thomson Digital

Printed in Singapore by Saik Wah Press Pte Ltd.

10 9 8 7 6 5 4 3 2

This book is dedicated to my parents, Peter and Amy
and my husband, Vincent

CONTENTS

PART I   PERSONAL   1

CHAPTER 1   HOW MONEY WORKS   3

CHAPTER 2   YOU CAN NEGOTIATE ANYTHING   25

CHAPTER 3   SPEAK SO PEOPLE WILL LISTEN   37

CHAPTER 4   IT'S WHO YOU KNOW   65

CHAPTER 5   IT IS BIGGER THAN YOU   75

PART II   OPERATIONS   85

CHAPTER 6   PROCESS   87

CHAPTER 7   HUMAN RESOURCES   101

CHAPTER 8   MARKETING   119

CHAPTER 9   SALES   141

CHAPTER 10   FINANCE   149

PART III   STRATEGY   159

CHAPTER 11   THE BIG PICTURE   161

CHAPTER 12   FILLING IN THE BLANKS   177

CHAPTER 13   ''PLANS ARE NOTHING. PLANNING IS EVERYTHING''   195

CHAPTER 14   THE CLASSICS   203
CHAPTER 15   FINAL WORDS   211

APPENDIX A   "WHY" AND "SO WHAT"   217

APPENDIX B   KEY INTERVIEWING TECHNIQUES
               FOR DATA COLLECTION   221

APPENDIX C   CAGR SHORTCUT   225

APPENDIX D   CHANGE MANAGEMENT
               TOOL: DICE   227

INDEX   229

PART I

PERSONAL

1

How Money Works

"Getting a Good Job Is a Dumb Idea"

Most parents and teachers would tell you: "Study hard in school, get a good job, receive a good salary, and live happily ever after." In fact, when I was a senior at Stanford, the only thing my friends could talk about was how to get a good job at a consulting firm or at an investment bank.

There is nothing wrong with getting a good job if you just want a stable life. A good job, by definition, pays well and has good career advancement opportunities. You will save up and eventually will be able to buy a nice place to live in, own a car, and send your kids to school. Although you will most likely always have to be careful with your expenditure to make sure you can pay the mortgage and the school bills, you will still be somewhat comfortable. You will most likely be in the good solid middle or slightly upper middle class.

However, to most Harvard Business School (HBS) students, "getting a good job" is a means, not an end. HBS students do not think of "getting a good job" as the ultimate goal for several reasons:

a. *If maximizing wealth is your ultimate goal, then salary is not the most efficient source of income.*

HBS teaches you to differentiate between two types of income: linear and investment. Linear income depends on how much time you put in. In a way, it is selling your time at a certain price per unit of time. Salary is a linear income. You put in one month and you get paid for that one month. No more, no less. The more valuable your time is because of your experience, competence, or tenure, the more you get paid per unit of time. But you stop getting paid the moment you stop work.

Investment income, on the other hand, does not depend on how much time you put in. You invest money (and maybe also some time to do due diligence and some follow-up) and you get continuous payoffs. Your income is not directly correlated with how much time you put in. The payoff is not a result of selling your time. Rental income, stock dividends, book royalties, and savings account interest, for example, are investment income streams. You put in money (and maybe some time) in the beginning and then you receive an income year after year. (Now a small test question: If you buy a small fruit shop and stand there selling fruit 12 hours a day, is your monthly income linear or is it an investment income? The answer is linear, because even though you are not working for a salary, if you stop working tomorrow, the fruit stand will have to cease business. But if you invest in the fruit stand and hire someone else to manage it while you just monitor the results as you see fit and pocket the profits, it is investment income).

Linear income is far inferior to investment income. After all, you stop generating linear income if you stop work. Linear income therefore is more risky. Also, you have only 24 hours a day. There is a limit to how much time you can put into your work. In fact, the secret of wealthy people is not only that they have more money but they also have more free time to enjoy life. Looking at wealth this way, many professionals are really not as wealthy as they appear. Doctors and dentists do not earn investment income from their profession. They have to keep seeing patients to earn money. If they take a year off, they have no income from their practice for the year. Also, the income level from their practice is more or less capped. There are only that many days a year and they can only see that many patients a day.

Of course, some jobs (such as major corporations, partnerships, or start-ups) give you stock options or outright grants of stock. This will mean your job now could generate investment income in addition to linear income. This is marvelous, but it should be noted that in major established corporations, employees have to be quite senior to get significant stock options. You may be able to get more stock options from start-ups. For example, I once met a wealthy HBS alumnus, and this was his story:

> I was one of the earlier employees of a start-up back in the late 1980s. It was very small when I was there. I got some stock options but I did not think much of them as I was not very senior and the value did not seem much. Then I left the company. After the company got listed some years later, I would check the newspaper once in a full moon on the stock price. For years, it always seemed to be about the same level every time I looked. So I would sigh and not pay attention. One day I decided to sell the shares as they were not going anywhere. It was then that I found out the company had had many stock splits over the years and my stocks were worth a lot of money.[1]

Unfortunately, start-ups give more stock options because they have a high risk of failure. When the start-up fails, its stock options will be worth nothing.

b. *If financial security is your ultimate goal, then working as an employee is risky.*

You can lose your job, even when you are performing very well. Poor economy, strong competition, office politics, and a dozen other factors can make you lose your job. Even blue chip companies often have to lay off good performers as well as bad during economic downturns. In *The Millionaire Mind*, Thomas J. Stanley reports surveying 733 millionaires in the United States and finding that most of these millionaires worked for themselves. Paraphrasing and combining the thoughts of several of these millionaires, the author describes how the millionaires responded to the idea of safety and security in working for a salary rather than for themselves:

> (Working for the others) may actually put you at greater risk . . . Having a single source of income . . . not being given the opportunity to learn how to make thousands of decisions . . . decisions you would have mastered if you were self-employed . . . you are not doing things that are in your own best (economic) interest for you to become successful in terms of becoming wealthy. . . . You are merely doing what is in the best interest of an employer.[2]

c. *If job satisfaction is your ultimate goal, then working as an employee may also be less than satisfactory.*

Office politics and the boss's temperament, policies, and rules often affect the job satisfaction that can be derived from work. One of my very good friends worked for a famous consulting firm's San Francisco office. He loves consulting work. He had always thought working for a major American consulting firm was his ideal job because he would get to work with top management of Fortune 500 companies even when he was just fresh out of business school. However, he quickly found he hated it. The key problem was the consulting company had a "free market" policy, which meant a project manager could choose the team members for a project. No transparency and no objective criteria. Project managers could choose whoever they wanted. So you can imagine what the environment was like. It was cutthroat and people would backstab, bad-mouth, and kiss up in an effort to get onto major projects. People would also do a lot of "face time"—hanging around the office till late in the night in order to look busy, to listen in to the latest gossip, and to "build relationships" whenever necessary. My friend quit after six months.

For all these reasons, many HBS graduates look at a job as a means, not an end. Many do work at a job, but they keep it in perspective. That is, they know why they are doing the job they are doing. Some HBS people look at their jobs mainly as a source of cash to fund their investments. They may like their jobs, but their goal is to maximize their salary to fund their investments. They spend much of their free time planning their investments.

In addition, most HBS people look at their jobs as an opportunity to learn, not just to earn. They want to learn to prepare themselves for when they own their own business (and generate investment income). They find jobs where they can learn and try to get new responsibilities all the time to acquire new skills. They do careful planning to ensure they are accumulating skills they need: industry expertise, management skills, financial tools, technical know-how, and the like. This is why so many HBS graduates go into consulting and management training programs. These jobs provide variety. Many HBS graduates consider changing jobs when they stop learning. This will help give them new skills and expand their social networks.

In addition, pay and number of years with the same company show an interesting relationship. You are always overpaid when you get a new job with new responsibilities. This is because you do not know much about the new job and you spend most of your time learning. But as soon as you stop learning, you are under, because you are now working just for the money and you are i. learning anymore. Of course, if you stay on and become very senio. and pretty much irreplaceable, you might become overpaid again.

HBS graduates also look for stock options wherever they work. They negotiate hard on the terms of the stock options. Basically, a stock option is the option to buy company stock at an agreed price (the *exercise price*) between a start date (the *option grant date*) and a deadline (the *expiry date*). The lower the exercise price, the earlier the start date, and the later the expiry date, the better. Stock options gain value over time as the stock price increases (a form of investment income). If converted into stocks, stock options would generate dividends (more investment income). If sold, stock options generate a chunk of cash that can be used to invest in other areas.

Cash as Your Ultimate Employee

Here is a very simple but powerful way to look at money: see each dollar as your employee. This idea is well captured in the best seller *Rich Dad, Poor Dad*: "The poor and the middle class work for money. The rich have money work for them."[3] You have to put your employees to work, that is, invest your money.

Another way is to see every dollar as a seed that can grow into a huge tree. This is the power of *compounding*. You probably already know about compound interest. It is similar to what banks tell you when they say your money will "grow" if you leave it with them. You leave the interest in the bank along with the original investment. Over time, the interest earned on the interest on your original investments makes your return multiply like a seed growing into a tree and tree developing more seeds and more trees. But of course, savings accounts provide one of the lowest rates of return. So how much is one of these seeds really worth at a higher rate of return? Well, if you invest a dollar a day at 20 percent return per annum, you get your first million after only 32 years. At $10 a day but 10 percent return a year, you still get your million in less than 35 years. This is the power of compounding! Albert Einstein is believed to have described compounding as the "greatest mathematical discovery of all times." Ben Franklin, one of the U.S. founding fathers, is believed to have described compound interest as "the stone that will turn lead into gold. . . . Money can beget money, and its offspring can beget more."[4]

Once you see cash as employees or as seeds that can grow into trees, you will of course want as much cash as possible. You will want to invest the cash so you can put the employees to work and grow the seeds into trees. So how to make sure you have as much cash as possible to invest? You can do so by clearly differentiating between investments and expenses, and by saving before spending on expenses.

An investment is something that generates or has the potential to generate cash income. An expense is something that will not generate cash. Investments turn cash into employees and get you more cash. Expenses mean you are killing your employees. For example:

Investment	Expense
Bonds	New car
Stocks	New LV bags, new Armani shirts, and so on
Real estate	Food, restaurants
Companies	Movies
Collectibles	Vacations
Your home	Your home

Why mention homes twice? Most people see their home as an investment. But what do they do?

- Instead of finding the best bargain, they pay market or even above-market price to buy the place they like most.
- Instead of buying in an area that has the most appreciation value, they buy in an area where they would like to live, even if it is an overbuilt and overpriced area.
- They spend excessive amounts on renovating and furnishing the place.
- They buy something that stretches their means. They take on a big debt. As a result, their monthly mortgage payment is so big that they do not have money left over to make other investments.

By contrast, early in their careers, most HBS graduates I know look at their home as an investment. They buy at discounted market price and then trade up when they can sell at a good price. They will exploit leverage wisely and make sure they have enough cash left over after paying their mortgage to make other investments. Then when they accumulate enough wealth, they buy their dream home.

Many people save whatever they have left after their expenses. But looking at cash as your employees, this would be like "first sacrifice the ones you need to kill and then try to put the leftover ones to work." It should be the other way round. You should always save to invest before you spend on expenses. In *The Richest Man in Babylon*, George S. Clayson highlighted one of the key success secrets of the ancients: "A part of all you earn is yours to keep."[5] But many people only save what is "left over." Prosperous people often save first and then live on what is left over. This makes a big difference. It not only makes sure you have cash to invest, it also forces you to plan your expenses and be more resourceful if you find that your cash after savings is not enough to cover your expenses.

POSSIBLE SOURCES OF INVESTMENT INCOME (I): REAL ESTATE

So if dollars are your employees, where should they be put to work? If each dollar is a seed, then how to grow the seeds into trees? In other words, where to invest?

Before discussing where to invest, it is important to first emphasize the difference between speculation and investment and to understand risk. Speculation is when you hope to get a return. Results are subject to chance and are out of your control. Gambling or buying lottery tickets is speculation. Buying real estate on the assumption that whatever you pick will increase in value over time is speculation (which is indeed one of the key root causes of the 2008 U.S. housing market and financial crisis). Investment is when you earn a return. You have a strategy and a plan. You do your research and analysis. You manage your investment accordingly to increase your chance of a return. HBS focuses on investing, not on speculating.

It is also important to understand risk. No one has a crystal ball. Even with all the research, analysis, and planning you can do, *when you invest, you always risk losing money*. As the saying goes, "no risk, no return." HBS does not teach you to minimize risk. This is because risk is often proportional to potential return. The key is not to minimize risk but to manage risk. Managing risk means you understand the risk involved and have determined that you can afford it, and the potential reward is worth the risk you are taking.

There are many possible sources of investment income. Three of my favorites are real estate, the public stock market, and private companies. Most HBS graduates I know invest in at least two and many in all three. Investing in multiple sources helps manage risk because of the safety of diversification and wider exposure to opportunities. To manage risks, most people start with simple, small investments and step by step move to more complex and larger deals as they become more experienced. I discuss real estate and the public stock market in this book, but not investing in private companies, which requires sophistication in deal sourcing, industry evaluation, company assessment, valuation, monitoring, and exit. It would take a whole book in itself to explain. Also, it is much riskier and often requires much bigger investments than real estate and the public stock market, though its returns can be substantially bigger.

First, consider real estate as a source of investment income. There is a famous story called "Acres of Diamonds" by Russell H. Conwell[6] about a man who dreamed of owning a diamond mine. He sold his farm, took the money, and wasted his life in a futile search. Ironically, the man who bought his farm was looking in the stream behind the farmhouse and noticed a brilliant, shiny stone glittering in the water. Yes, it was a diamond. Thus was discovered the famous diamond mine from which came many of the crown jewels in Europe. The farm was sitting atop acres of diamonds.

Many people are like the man going in search of diamonds. They waste time, money, and energy in endless moneymaking schemes while the greatest source of wealth is under their feet—real estate. If you look at people who are filthy rich, real estate is close to being a common denominator. People such as Donald Trump, Li Ka Shing, and many other billionaires around the world made their fortunes in real estate. Of course, many of them started off with a lot of money and they invested millions of dollars. However the beauty of real estate is that you do not really have to be a major developer. You can start with a small amount of money on small properties and gradually expand.

The attractiveness of real estate comes from a number of key factors:

- Leverage
- Multiple sources of cash flow
- Bargains

Leverage

Archimedes said, "Give me a lever and I'll move to earth." As investors, we do not want to use the lever to move the world; we just want to use it to buy as much as we can. In the finance world, *lever*, or *leverage*, means borrowing. Because you have to pay interest to borrow, many people wrongly believe you borrow only when you cannot afford to pay all cash. HBS teaches you to use leverage even when you can easily afford to pay all in your own cash. Leverage allows you to increase the amount you earn for each dollar you invest (percentage return). In a way, if cash is your employee, leverage is like borrowing employees from someone else to work for you. You pay for the use of these temporary employees, but they help you achieve more with less of your own workforce.

An example to illustrate of how leverage can improve profitability: say you buy an apartment that is worth US$200,000. The apartment is expected to appreciate 10 percent in one year. You can obtain a loan at 5 percent interest a year. Assuming you can afford to pay US$200,000 in your own cash, would you pay all with your own cash or would you borrow?

Here is the math. Assuming no fees and taxes, if you pay all cash, you make 10 percent on your money invested after one year. But if you take a loan of 80 percent and pay only 20 percent in cash, you would make 30 percent on your money invested:

Selling price (10 percent appreciation)	220,000
Minus interest paid	8,000
Minus mortgage repayment	160,000
Minus 20 percent deposit paid	40,000
Net profit	12,000
Percent returns	30 percent
	(12,000/40,000)

Of course, while leverage is powerful, overleveraging is extremely dangerous, as evidenced by the 2008 sub-prime mortgage crisis; I'll return to this point shortly.

Now, you may argue that if you invest without borrowing and make 10 percent, you make $20,000, which is higher than $12,000. This is true but then you run the risk of "too many eggs in one basket." HBS teaches that while many analytical tools can help you understand the markets, no one really has a crystal ball. One HBS graduate I know works for a famous investment bank. He works as a research analyst, writing reports widely read by fund managers around the world. Each report analyzes a particular company and makes recommendation on whether to buy, hold, or sell the stock of the company. I still remember this classic quote: he said, "I am doing well in the firm. I am right about one-third of the time, wrong about one-third, and the rest is neither right nor wrong because the unexpected happens." Well, so much for predicting the market.

So if no one really knows for sure what is going to happen in the market, what do you do? HBS teaches you to diversify. If you invest your $200,000 cash in five different apartments of about the same price range, putting down 20 percent of your cash as deposit for each and borrowing 80 percent for each, you would generate 30 percent return on your $200,000 instead of 10 percent. You will also be diversifying your risk. Even if you lose on one apartment, you may still be able to make up by success in your other apartments. Instead of investing only in real estate, you can also diversify by investing in other areas like bonds, public stocks, or even collectibles or private businesses.

Multiple Sources of Cash Flow Over Time

The second reason why real estate is attractive is the multiple streams of investment income it can generate:

- Rent
- Loan reduction
- Value appreciation
- Tax deductions

Cash Flow from Rent

To calculate this cash flow, use the following formula:

Income from rent	
Minus	Operating expenses (rates, tax, maintenance, management fees, and so on)
Minus	Loan repayment
Net cash flow	

As can be seen in the formula, cash flow is a direct function of the loan repayment. The bigger the loan you take and the shorter the repayment period, the smaller the net cash flow until the loan is paid off. So how much loan should one take to maximize returns? To calculate, use the following formula:

$$\frac{\text{Net cash flow}}{\text{Cash investment}} = \% \text{ cash-on-cash returns}$$

The final decision on how much debt to take on should be based on both percent cash-on-cash returns and the risk involved in the loans. Negative cash flow will happen if the related expenses and loan payments are greater than the rental income, especially since the property would inevitably have no income from time to time as a result of tenant turnover. You must be able to cover that negative cash flow through your net cash flow generated in the past, your salary, or your other investment income. Many people in Hong Kong were forced into bankruptcy after 1997 because they did not plan their cash flow well. They accepted negative net cash flow (rental income that did not cover mortgage payments and expenses) because they believed they could profit when the property appreciated. But property prices continued to fall for a few years after 1997. When some of these people lost their jobs in the 2001/2002 recession, they could no longer make their monthly payments to the banks. Neither could they get cash by selling the property, because property prices had declined so much that the price they could get by selling would be less than what they owed the bank (this is called *negative equity*). As a result, these people were forced into mortgage defaults or even personal bankruptcy. Overleveraging and negative equity are also key contributors to the 2008 global financial crisis. Hence, while leverage is powerful in increasing profits, you must look at your own financial situation to determine how much you should borrow.

Cash Flow from Loan Reduction

Over time, as you pay down the principal of your mortgage, your equity (your ownership of the property net of debt) will grow.

You can get cash from this increase in equity in two ways: sell or refinance. Selling is straightforward but may not be the best thing to do unless you have a better investment than the property in hand. Refinancing is another option. For example, say you purchased an apartment with 20 percent deposit. Your equity was 20 percent then. Over time, you paid down your loan and your equity increased. Say your equity has grown to 65 percent after 10 years, and assume the value of the property has not changed, and you can refinance and get a new loan for 80 percent of the value of your property. You repay the 35 percent (100 percent minus 65 percent) you owe on your earlier loan. You can use the remaining 45 percent (80 percent minus 35 percent) to make other investments or to indulge yourself by spending on expenses.

Figure 1.1   North American Home Prices

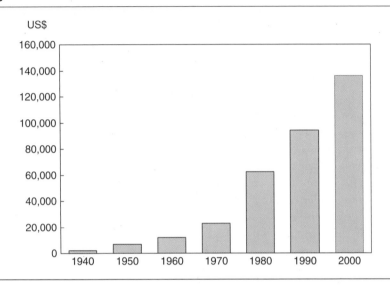

Source: U.S. government statistics.

Cash Flow from Value Appreciation

Among all the lessons history teaches, none is more certain than the fact that real estate will appreciate in the long-term. Figure 1.1 shows what happened to the median price of homes in North America between 1940 and 2000.

Some experts may disagree. Throughout history, there have been many self-proclaimed experts who predicted that "real estate prices have peaked." Take a look what experts have been saying in the United States during these 60 years (as collected by Gary W. Eldred in *The 106 Common Mistakes Homebuyers Make*):[7]

- The prices of houses seem to have reached a plateau, and there is reasonable expectancy that prices will decline. (*Time*, December 1947)
- Home cost is too much for the mass market. Today's average price is around $8,000, out of reach for two-thirds of all buyers. (*Science Digest*, April 1948)
- If you have bought your house since the War . . . you have made your deal at the top of the market. . . . The days when you couldn't lose on a house purchase are no longer with us. (*House Beautiful*, November 1948)

- The goal of owning a home seems to be getting beyond the reach of more and more Americans. The typical new house today is about $28,000. (*BusinessWeek*, September 1969)
- The median price of a home today is approaching $50,000. Housing experts predict price rises in the future won't be that great. (*Nation's Business*, June 1977)
- The era of easy profits in real estate may be drawing to a close. (*Money*, January 1981)
- In California . . . for example, it is not unusual to find families of average means buying $100,000 houses. . . . I'm confident prices have passed their peak. (John Wesley English and Gray Emerson Cardiff, *The Coming Real Estate Crash*, 1980)
- The golden-age of risk-free run-ups in home prices is gone. (*Money*, March 1985)
- If you're looking to buy, be careful. Rising home values are not a sure thing anymore. (*Miami Herald*, October 1985)
- Most economists agree . . . (a home) will become little more than a roof and a tax deduction, certainly not the lucrative investment it was through much of the 1980s. (*Money*, April 1986)
- Financial planners agree that houses will continue to be a poor investment. (*Kiplinger's Personal Financial Magazine*, November 1993)
- A home is where a bad investment is. (*San Francisco Examiner*, November 1996)

However, history has proven these experts (and many others) wrong. Data indicate that over the *long-term*, real estate *generally* increases in value. I emphasize *long-term* (10 or 20 years or even more) because there will be short- to medium-term ups and downs due to economic cycles and turmoil, but real estate prices tend to go up over the long-term. Of course, it will be years before we can see how the 2008 U.S. housing market crash will play out. But data on median prices so far still seem to indicate that while median price in the United States has declined roughly 20 percent from the peak (around 2005 and 2006), it is still higher in 2008 than it was 10 or 20 years ago.

I also emphasize *generally* because this does not mean every property will appreciate. Appreciation of an individual property depends on its location, condition, management, purchase price, and other factors. As with any investment (not speculation), you must be prepared to put in time to research and understand the market.

Property generally appreciates for two main reasons: inflation and supply versus demand. While economic growth is cyclical and deflation sometimes occurs, prices generally inflate over the long-term. When there is inflation, prices go up, including those of property.

While it is definitely true that modest inflation over the long-term increases home prices, some people mistakenly believe that the higher the inflation, the greater the increase in price. The logic of high inflation goes like this: with inflation and hence rapidly rising prices for labor and materials, developers cut back on new construction and raise prices. With higher prices for new development, many property buyers switch to the resale market and buy existing homes. With more buyers bidding for existing property, the prices go up.

However, this high inflation, high property appreciation is not so true anymore. The key reason is the way central banks in many countries are now using interest rates to control inflation. Interest rates are often raised when inflation becomes too high. As interest rates go up, home affordability goes down. People who might like to buy are blocked from the market. On the other hand, low rates of inflation mean low interest rates. With low mortgage interest, more people can afford to buy. More demand means higher prices. Therefore, real estate prices may continue to go up even in a low-inflation environment.

Cash Flow from Tax Deductions

In many countries, the government encourages home ownership through various tax deductions. Different countries have different tax deduction allowances. Here are some of the items qualified for tax deductions in various countries:

- Purchase costs such as prepaid interest on the loan, fire and liability insurance, escrow fees, or miscellaneous fees from lender.
- Ongoing operating expenses such as interest on loans, insurance, utilities, gardening and cleaning expenses, repairs such as roofing or plumbing, or management fees.
- Depreciation. In some countries such as the United States, property owners are given an annual depreciation allowance on the structure (that is, the building but not the land) to deduct against other income. The theory is that this deduction will be saved up and will be used to replace the structure at the end of its useful life. This is similar to depreciation of equipment for businesses.

Tax deductions increase property owners' cash flows by reducing the amount of taxes they have to pay on their income. This is especially significant in countries where income tax is extremely high.

Bargains

One key concept about investing I took away from HBS: "Often, you do not make money when you sell. You make money when you buy." Warren Buffett preaches the same phenomenon: buy at bargain price so you have a margin of safety. Then, even if the market does not appreciate as forecast, you will have built in a buffer because you buy below market price. You may still be able to make a profit (or at least not lose as much money) when you sell. Many people made millions speculating in the Hong Kong property market prior to 1997, but many have gone bankrupt since then. Prices were rising so rapidly prior to 1997 that many people were buying at market prices without bothering to look for bargains, so they had no leeway when the market paused.

One of the key attractions of real estate is the possibility of finding bargains. Bargains are available for three reasons. First, relative to the stock market, where sellers can find buyers at market price with relatively little effort (just call the stockbroker), the property market is relatively illiquid. "Willing" or desperate property sellers may not easily find buyers. They may consent to drop prices just to close a deal quickly (of course, at the same time, such illiquidity might affect you if you need to sell quickly). Second, property is not a commodity like stock. Each property is different (location, floor level, view, condition, number of bedrooms). Hence there is room for negotiation depending on the property seller's level of desperation, knowledge of the market, and negotiation skills relative to those of the buyer. Third, some property owners do not manage their property well. They do not maintain and configure according to market needs. As a result, there is opportunity to buy such property and then quickly increase the value by renovation (new paint, new pipes, new carpet or floor tiles, an additional bedroom, and the like).

So the key is to find a bargain by identifying either a willing seller or a seller who has not been managing the property very well. By finding bargains and paying below market price, you can be more certain about locking in profit. There are many reasons why a property owner becomes a willing seller: relocation to another city, needing money for another investment or expense, time constraints, debt (including foreclosures by banks), divorce, sickness, or a hundred other factors. A property owner may not be managing the property well due to lack of time, interest, cash, or expertise.

Leverage, multiple streams of cash flow, and availability of bargains are three of the key advantages of real estate investing. There are two strategies in real estate investing: buy and sell quickly (flip) and long-term hold. The former is more risky. Most of the cash flow from flipping will be from value appreciation. Hence flipping requires more sophistication because you need to find bargains and know how to upgrade the property to increase the market value. Just buying at market price and hoping to sell at a much higher value quickly is a risky, speculative strategy. Long-term hold is relatively less risky as you can get multiple streams of cash flow.

POSSIBLE SOURCES OF INVESTMENT INCOME (II): PUBLIC STOCKS

Three key questions will guide you to investing in stocks: which stock, when to invest, and when to get out.

Which Stock to Invest In?

HBS offers multiple courses on finance. We spent months learning advanced concepts and techniques for valuing companies (and hence their stocks). But during the very last class of the course, one of my classmates, a very experienced banker, made a comment:

> All these techniques are useful tools. But if you plan to use them to pick individual stocks, you should know this data I have read: 75 percent of all the smartest money managers in the world, working 20-hour days, with huge research staffs and the most advanced computers, have not been able to consistently beat the market averages. Of the remaining 25 percent, most were just able to keep pace with the market average. Only a handful of the rest (including Warren Buffett) have beaten the market consistently. But even for these few, many have beaten the market on average over a long-term, not if you look at short-term year by year.

I was shocked to hear this. I later found out from him that he had picked up the information from the book *Multiple Streams of Income*.[8] The book provided further research evidence that in the years from 1990 to 2000 in the United States, out of over 6,000 professionally managed mutual funds, only 20 were able to outperform the market average after expenses and fees.[9] Look at all the stock market commentators and so-called gurus around you—if they are so smart in picking stocks, they should be millionaires by now. Why are they still hosting radio shows and writing newspaper columns or research reports?

So what should you do? You can do one of two things. As mentioned earlier, there is a handful of Warren Buffetts around. You can invest in the funds they manage, but this could be tricky. First, past performance is not a guarantee of future performance. Past performance is not even a guarantee of future performance these days, as the people who invested with Bernie Madoff have learned at their cost. Second, Warren Buffett and a number of the other stars like him are quite old. So there is always the risk that their funds may significantly deteriorate after they retire. Third, some of these funds are not so easily accessible. Warren Buffett's fund, Berkshire Hathaway, is traded only in the United States and at a high per-share price.

The second option is to invest in market average (stock market indexes such as the S&P 500 index fund or Tracker fund in Hong Kong). Most markets include investment funds that will track an index. They aim at providing the same return as the index by buying and holding all the stocks that make up the index. While it would be very difficult, if not impossible, to beat the market average by trying to pick individual stocks, you can still make a handsome profit if your investment performs at market average. Over the long-term (more than 10 years), the United States stock market index S&P 500 averages an annual return of 10 percent over 15 percent. Not a bad rate if you remember the principle of compounding covered earlier in this book.

This is why many HBS graduates invest in stock index funds. Of course, given the great ego many HBS graduates have, many still invest in investment funds and individual stocks. They either believe they can pick the 20 winners out of the 6,000-plus funds or believe they have enough information to pick individual stocks. But the risk involved in picking the right ones and the higher certainty of the index funds make stock indexes a better investment for most people. Also, index funds charge much lower management fees than other types of investment funds since index funds do not require research and have lower *churn rates* (the buying and selling of securities by fund managers, which incur commission costs and possibly taxes in some countries).

When to Sell

It may seem illogical, but it's useful to tackle this question first, before going back to "when to buy." Many people try to time the market. There is nothing wrong with a "buy low, sell high" strategy, except for the extreme difficulty of consistently timing the short-term highs and lows accurately. For example, in the 10 years 1980 to 1989, the S&P 500 index gained over 17 percent per year, with frequent short-term ups and downs. During this period, there were about 2,528 trading days. Almost 30 percent of the entire profit for the decade was generated in just 10 days. If you had tried to "buy low and sell high" but happened to miss those 10 days out of the 2,528, you would have lost almost 30 percent of your gain for the entire decade![10]

It is difficult if not impossible to forecast the day-to-day or year-to-year ups and downs because stock prices are driven not only by business fundamentals but also by investors' sentiment. Ben Graham, widely known as the Father of Financial Analysis and teacher to Warren Buffett, emphasized this element of emotion by comparing the stock market with an allegorical character he created called "Mr. Market." Buffett shared this story with his investors in the 1987 annual report of his investment company Berkshire Hathaway. The story goes like this: imagine that you and Mr. Market are partners in a private business. Every day Mr. Market offers a price at which he is willing to either buy your shares in the business or sell you his. Although the business that you own jointly is a stable, predictable business, Mr. Market's offers are rather unstable and often unpredictable. Some days, Mr. Market will offer a very high price because he is optimistic and cheerful. This could be because interest rates are down or another company announces good results or a war has ended and he can only see bright days ahead. On other days, Mr. Market can be very pessimistic and offers a very low price.

So what should you do? Should you be optimistic when Mr. Market is optimistic and be pessimistic when Mr. Market feels down? Graham believed that Mr. Market is very much like the real-life stock market, when short-term market prices are often driven by emotions that are irrational and ephemeral.

This is why Warren Buffett, one of the most famous investors in our time, has made his position on forecasting very clear in his books and speeches: Don't waste your time. Whether it is the economy, the interest rates, the market, or individual stock prices, Buffett believes that forecasting these parameters is futile. But Buffett does not say the future is unpredictable. Two things about the future are certain:

- The market will eventually reward great companies by increasing their stock price. But no one knows exactly when this will happen.
- In the short-term, stock prices will always be volatile because of emotional factors, and because there will always be many speculators trying to predict short-term ups and downs.

So what does Warren Buffett do? He invests in great companies and holds them for the long-term. He does not care about any short-term price fluctuation. He will patiently wait as he is certain that the great companies he selects will eventually be rewarded. In fact, Buffett sees temporary price decline as an opportunity to buy more shares in the great companies in his portfolio.

The same approach applies to investing in stock market indexes. Figure 1.2 shows the long-term trend of the S&P 500 of the United States.

History suggests stock market indexes increase over the long run. This is because indexes are made up of a basket of companies, and over the long-term, the good ones will get rewarded and the poor ones get eliminated from the indexes.

But indexes are going to fluctuate in the short-term, just like individual stocks. In the 50 years between 1950 and 1999, there were 11 years when the S&P 500 recorded a decline. That is roughly one losing year every five years. So if you buy in any one year during this period, and

- Sell after one year, then your odds of winning will be roughly 80 percent (four out of five). Not bad, but still relatively high risk.
- Sell after five years, then your odds increase to 85 percent.
- Sell after 10 years, then your odds become 95 percent.
- Sell after 25 years, then your odds of winning are almost 100 percent![11]

Figure 1.2 U.S. Stock Market (S&P 500), 1950–2007

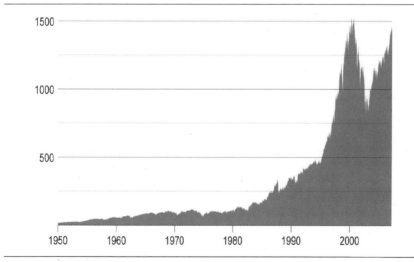

Source: Daily closings (S&P 500).

So the answer to "when to sell" is somewhere between 10 and 25 years. In fact, I have heard Buffett quoted as saying, "My favorite holding period is . . . forever."

When to Buy?

If the key is to hold for a long period of time, then the time to buy is as soon as possible. The sooner you buy, the longer you have your money (employees) at work, and the more money you have to compound. If you fully subscribe to the theory that you cannot time the market, then the time to buy will be this moment, since you will not know when the next dip is.

But still, it is in human nature to at least try to wait until the next market dip. You feel you may overpay if you just rush out and buy an index fund right now. There is a sophisticated yet very simple strategy called dollar cost averaging that I find very useful in reducing the risk and anxiety. This strategy is also useful if, like most people, you do not really have a lot of cash lying around or you are new to this idea and would like to try out with small amounts of money at a time.

Dollar cost averaging goes like this. You set a fixed amount you want to invest in a selected index every month. If the price is high in a certain month, your fixed amount of money will buy a smaller number of shares. If the price is low that month, the same amount of money will buy more shares. So over long periods, the average purchase price of your holdings is less than the market average price. Table 1.1 is an example comparing dollar cost averaging (investing the same $ amount each month, say $1,000 a month) to the strategy of buying the same number of shares each month regardless of price (say 50 shares a month for this example).

This shows how dollar cost averaging gives a lower average price per share, hence a bigger profit. In fact, dollar cost averaging would still have generated a profit even if the ending price falls to $18 per share. Dollar cost averaging is even more profitable if there are significant temporary market slumps once in a while as shown in Table 1.2.

This is because the fixed, predetermined sum is able to purchase a greater number of shares during these times, hence reducing average per-share price and increasing profit in the long-term when market recovers. Therefore, dollar cost averaging requires perseverance during poor market conditions. Its advantages will be limited if it is only practiced during a strong market.

Again (I promise this is the last time I mention this in this book), I must emphasize that there is always a risk in any investment. Obviously, dollar cost

Table 1.1 Dollar Cost Averaging Example 1

	January	February	March	April	May	June	Total	Average Cost per Share
Market price per share	20	18	16	16	18	21		18.17
Fixed number strategy								
– number of shares purchased	50	50	50	50	50	50	300	18.17
– $ invested	1000	900	800	800	900	1050	5450	
Dollar cost average (same $ strategy)								
– $ invested	1000	1000	1000	1000	1000	1000	6000	17.98
– number of shares purchased	50	56	63	63	56	48	334	

averaging assumes a long-term appreciation (or a slight decline at most) of the stock market. While this has always been true before, it may not be true for overheated markets or for newly developed markets that may run into a major market correction that never recovers.

Table 1.2 Dollar Cost Averaging Example 2

	January	February	March	April	May	June	Total	Average Cost per Share
Market price per share	20	18	5	5	18	21		14.50
Fixed number strategy								
– number of shares purchased	50	50	50	50	50	50	300	14.50
– $ invested	1000	900	250	250	900	1050	4350	
Dollar cost average (same $ strategy)								
– $ invested	1000	1000	1000	1000	1000	1000	6000	9.86
– number of shares purchased	50	56	200	200	56	48	609	

Notes

1. A stock split increases the number of shares outstanding by issuing more shares to current shareholders. Price per share is reduced accordingly, so the total value of all outstanding shares remains the same. For example, say a company has 1,000 shares of stock outstanding at $50 per share. The total value of the outstanding stocks is 1,000 × $50, or $50,000. The company splits its stock 2 for 1. There are now 2,000 shares and each shareholder owns twice as many shares. The price of each share is adjusted to $25. The total value is now 2,000 × $25 = $50,000, the same as before. Companies tend to split stock if the price has increased significantly and is perceived to be too expensive for small investors.
2. Thomas J. Stanley, *The Millionaire Mind* (Kansas City: Andrews McMeel, 2001), 135.
3. Robert T. Kiyosaki and Sharon L. Lechter, *Rich Dad, Poor Dad* (New York: Business Plus, 2000), 46.
4. V. P. Sriraman, "*The Power of Compounding*," Bharathidasan School of Management; available online: www.bim.edu/pdf/lead_article/compounding.pdf (access date: January 12, 2009).
5. George S. Clayson, *The Richest Man in Babylon* (New York: Signet, 1998), 21.
6. Conwell is best remembered as the founder and first president of Temple University in Philadelphia, Pennsylvania. His famous story, "Acres of Diamonds," is available online: www.temple.edu/about/Acres_of_Diamonds.htm (access date: January 12, 2009).
7. Gary W. Eldred, *The 106 Common Mistakes Homebuyers Make* (New York: Wiley, 1995), 38–39.
8. Robert G. Allen, *Multiple Streams of Income* (New York: Wiley, 2000), 51.
9. Ibid., 54.
10. Ibid., 57.
11. Ibid., 53.

2

YOU CAN NEGOTIATE

ANYTHING

YOU ARE CONSTANTLY NEGOTIATING

Like it or not, you are a negotiator. Negotiation is a fact of life. Governments negotiate treaties. Businesses negotiate deals and contracts. You negotiate with your boss on your salary. You negotiate with strangers to purchase a house, a car, or even just a T-shirt from a street vendor. You negotiate with your kids on how late they can stay up. You negotiate with your spouse on how often you should see your in-laws. Negotiation is the basic tool for getting a solution when you and the other side have some shared and opposing interests. HBS devotes much time to negotiation skills.

In this chapter, I highlight some of the key concepts taught at HBS, which I have found very useful in my personal and professional life. It is crucial to understand the other parties' real interest and best alternative if they do not reach an agreement, to help reframe the context and terms of the negotiation. Once the stage is set, the key soft skills to get the other side to agree are careful listening and building a "golden bridge."

UNDERSTAND THE OTHER PARTIES' REAL INTEREST

This is a story I heard from an HBS classmate: Years ago, when China was negotiating to enter the World Trade Organization (WTO), one of the key barriers was whether China should enter as a developing or a developed country. China insisted on joining as a developing country, but a number of other countries disagreed. The two positions were incompatible and it appeared that one side would have to be forced or persuaded to yield. But a solution was made possible once the parties looked at the real interests behind these positions. China wanted to join as a developing country because of the more favorable terms such as slower pace of market liberalization and bigger subsidies to certain sectors. Other countries wanted more demanding terms in some sectors, mostly to protect their own interests. Once this was understood, then instead of arguing developing versus developed, negotiations were refocused on the pace of liberalization and sector subsidies. Instead of sticking to standard terms related to developing versus developed countries, WTO members and China were able to work out China-specific terms in each area.

Another example is this well-known incident cited in many negotiation books. In 1978, President Sadat of Egypt and Prime Minister Begin of Israel met at Camp David to negotiate a peace treaty. They had to agree on the boundary between their countries but they were deadlocked because their positions were incompatible. Both sides wanted the Sinai Peninsula, which falls between the two countries. No matter how the boundaries were drawn and redrawn, no solution could be reached.

However a solution was made possible once the parties started looking at the real interests behind their positions. Egypt wanted sovereignty: Sinai had been part of Egypt since ancient times. Israel did not care about sovereignty over Sinai. It wanted Sinai because it did not want the Egyptian army to be anywhere close to the "real" Israeli border. It wanted Sinai to act as a buffer between the Egyptian border and the "real" Israel.

So although the positions were incompatible, the interests were not. In the end, a solution was successfully negotiated. Sinai was returned to complete Egyptian sovereignty but would be largely demilitarized to give Israel its military buffer zone.

These two examples illustrate the importance of understanding real interests. Then negotiation becomes a quest to find a solution that satisfies these interests as much as possible to get to a win-win situation. Failing to understand interests will result in "position negotiation." Each side takes an opposing position (China wanted to enter WTO as a developing country and a number of other countries wanted it to enter as a developed country.) Then negotiation becomes a zero-sum game—one party wins only if the other party gives in.

A classic story often cited to expose the weakness of position negotiation is the breakdown of the talks between the United States and the then Soviet Union on a ban of nuclear testing in both countries during John F. Kennedy's presidency. Both sides were agreeable to the idea of introducing a ban, which was a significant step. But to make sure the ban was enforced, they needed to agree on the number of annual on-site inspections each side would be allowed to make on the other's territory to investigate suspicious seismic events.

The United States insisted on no less than 10 inspections a year, but the Soviet Union would agree to three at most. The two positions could not be reconciled and the talks failed. In hindsight, some negotiation experts believed an agreement could have been reached if the two sides had put their positions aside and focused on their interests by trying to work out a mutually acceptable definition of *inspection*. The experts pointed out that the negotiators never fully clarified what "an inspection" would involve—would it be a small team of inspectors going to the other country for a specific, limited time, focusing only on investigating suspicious seismic events, or would it be hundreds of inspectors allowed to pry indiscriminately for an extended period? Many negotiation experts felt that a well-defined inspection guideline and procedure balancing the interests of effective enforcement of the ban and protection of national security could have led to a successful solution.

So how do you understand the other party's interest? Ask and listen. Ask other people who have knowledge of the other party or similar situations elsewhere (benchmarking). Even ask the other party directly. In many negotiations, real interest is not that confidential. The other side may be willing to discuss what is important and what is not important to them.

Besides asking the others, put yourself in the other party's shoes and ask yourself, "Why are they asking for this or that? Why are they not agreeing to what I am offering? What would I like and not like if I were in their shoes?" An example of this is how Microsoft won the browser war in 1996. At that time, Netscape and Microsoft were both negotiating with AOL to be the service's browser partner. Netscape was the technology leader. Microsoft was relatively weak in technology. So instead of focusing the negotiation on technology, Microsoft figured out an even more important "hot button" for AOL—Microsoft offered to place an AOL icon on the Windows desktop right next to the icon for MSN, Microsoft's own online service, which directly competed with AOL. Hence, instead of focusing on the "obvious interest" of technology, Microsoft was able to identify the even more important interest through thinking from the other party's perspective.

However, while many situations are negotiable, that does not mean you should negotiate all the time. Even when you choose to negotiate, you do not necessarily use the "real interest" approach every time. Sometimes positional negotiation with give-and-take could suffice. This is because negotiation, especially "real interest" negotiation, takes effort and time.

Is it worth the time and effort to negotiate? Is it worth the time and effort to explore "real interests"? Different people have different views on their time and effort. I love haggling on price (which is a form of negotiation) with street vendors when I am on vacation in developing countries. I haggle even over items as low as US$2 or US$3. This is because I just hate overpaying. I hate being taken for a ride. So I feel it is worth my time and effort, but my haggling drives my husband crazy. He feels the time and effort could be better spent elsewhere.

KNOW THE BATNA

Using the "real interest" approach helps identify a win-win agreement. Understanding the importance of the "Best Alternative to a Negotiated Agreement" (BATNA) can help you maximize the win for your side. The advantage in negotiations often does not depend on how big and powerful each party is, but on who has a better BATNA: who can better afford to walk away without an agreement.

The power of BATNA is seen in everyday life. When supply is less than demand, the seller has a strong BATNA. If you won't agree to a price, many other customers will do so. In a depressed economy where supply is more than demand, buyers have all the leverage. They can always buy from another seller if they cannot get the price they want. Even toddlers understand BATNA; when they scream in a restaurant, they capitalize on an intuitive sense that their parents must either yield to their demands or risk more embarrassment and inconvenience.

The power of BATNA is also seen in more complex business situations. A classic example is the battle between Sky Television and British Satellite

Broadcasting (BSB) in the early 1990s to dominate British satellite television. It would be a lose-lose situation if both firms were to stay in the market and compete vigorously. It would be a win-win if they could negotiate a deal for one to pay the other to exit. These are the estimates for the financial implications as documented in a HBS case study:[1]

For BSB: Loss of £190 million if both BSB and Sky stay in game and fight; profit of more than £2 billion if Sky exits; loss of £180 million if BSB exits.

For Sky Television: Gain of £700 million if both parties stay in game and fight; profit of almost £3 billion if BSB exits; loss of £70 million if Sky exits.

Figure 2.1 displays the financials in a 2 × 2 matrix.

It would be a win-win if they could negotiate a deal for one to pay the other to exit. But who has a stronger negotiating position in this example? Some would say Sky has a stronger position, since it would still make £700 million even if BSB does not exit the market. BSB is weaker because it would lose £180–£190 million if Sky chooses to fight. So BSB must negotiate for Sky to exit.

However, that is not true if you look at the BATNA more carefully. Compare the fight versus exit option for each company if they fail to reach an agreement. If no agreement is reached for one of the players to exit, then:

For BSB: Fight versus exit means losing £190 million instead of £180 million. The difference is relatively insignificant. So BSB has flexibility of choosing whether to fight or not should Sky decide to fight. It has a strong BATNA.

For Sky: Fight versus exit means £700 million profit compared to a £70 million loss!

Figure 2.1 Comparing Results

	BSB fights	BSB exits
Sky fights	BSB loses £190 million Sky makes £700 million	BSB loses £180 million Sky makes almost £3 billion
Sky exits	BSB makes £2 billion Sky loses £70 million	Not possible (BSB and Sky will not both exit)

Sky has no choice but to fight. If it has to fight, then it will increase its profit substantially (from £700 million to £3 billion) if it can negotiate to pay BSB to exit. In fact, theoretically, if BSB does its homework and understands Sky's BATNA, it would know that Sky should be willing to pay anything up to £2.3 billion for BSB to exit! In the end, Sky did pay BSB to exit the market.

While sometimes the BATNAs for both sides are more or less fixed (as in the Sky/BSB case), many times a BATNA can be changed. Here are some of the most effective levers for changing BATNAs:

- Improve your own BATNA by creating competition.
- Weaken the other side's BATNA by adding parties that can increase the threat of negative consequences to no agreement.
- Weaken the other side's BATNA by teaming up with the BATNAs themselves!

Create Competition

This is intuitive: when you are a seller, you want to have many alternative buyers; when you are a buyer, you want to have many alternative suppliers. In the HBS case "Strategic Deal-Making at Millennium Pharmaceuticals,"[2] Steve Holtzman, ex-chief business officer, explains how the company's negotiation strategy helped grow it from a small start-up to a multibillion-dollar company in less than 10 years:

> Whenever we feel there's a possibility of a deal with someone, we immediately call six other people. It drives you nuts, trying to juggle them all. But number one, it will change the perception on the other side of the table. And two, it will change your self-perception. If you believe that there are other people who are interested, your bluff is no longer a bluff; it's real. It will come across with a whole other level of conviction.

It should also be noted that sometimes it could pay to become someone's BATNA. A few years ago, my small investment fund was invited to submit a proposal to bid for the development of a piece of land in Hong Kong. The property was only average in attractiveness and chances of winning were slim since many believed one of the leading property firms (call it Company C) was determined to win the bid. Therefore, we felt we could not justify putting in our time and resources to draft a high-quality proposal. When we called the seller to decline the invitation, the seller actually offered to compensate us for putting the proposal together in case we did not win. At that point, we realized we were being used as a BATNA: a bargaining chip for the seller. Company C had spread the word on its determination to win the bid and no other company wanted to waste resources competing.

Another example of improving BATNA through generating competition: when I was about to graduate from Stanford, I interviewed with the Boston Consulting Group (BCG) and got the offer. I thought the terms of the offer were standard. Since BCG was my first choice, I thought I should stop interviewing with other firms. But I quickly found out from some Stanford alumni already working in consulting that often, even though the key terms were standardized, other issues such as location and mentor assignment could be negotiated. In general, the more competing job offers a candidate had, the more a consulting firm saw the competition for getting the candidate, and the harder they would try to get the candidate to accept the offer. When I found out, I quickly changed my strategy and worked hard on my other interviews. (And I tactfully let BCG know I was doing that!)

Weaken the Other Side

It can help your case to add parties who increase the other side's exposure to negative consequences if they do not come to an agreement. When I was working at BCG, Seagram's was one of my clients. I heard many times the story of how Edgar Bronfman, the former CEO there, won a very unlikely negotiation against the Swiss banks. David A. Lax and Professor James K. Sebenius cite the same example:[3]

> When Edgar Bronfman, former CEO of Seagram's and head of the World Jewish Congress, first approached Swiss banks asking them to compensate Holocaust survivors whose families' assets had been unjustly held since World War II, he felt stonewalled. Swiss banking executives saw no reason to be forthcoming with Bronfman; they believed they were on strong legal ground because the restitution issue had been settled years ago. After eight months of lobbying by Bronfman, the World Jewish Congress, and others, the negotiations were dramatically expanded—to the detriment of the Swiss. The bankers faced a de facto coalition of interests that credibly threatened the lucrative Swiss share of the public finance business in states such as California and

New York. They faced the divestiture by huge U.S. pension funds of stock in Swiss banks as well as in all Swiss-based companies; a delay in the merger between Swiss Bank and UBS over the "character fitness" license vital to doing business in New York; expensive and intrusive lawsuits brought by some of the most formidable U.S. class-action attorneys; and the wider displeasure of the U.S. government, which had become active in brokering a settlement.

Given the bleak BATNA the Swiss faced, the bankers yielded and the parties reached an agreement, including a commitment from the Swiss bankers to pay US$1.25 billion to survivors. It was an "almost unimaginable outcome" at the beginning of the negotiation when "the Swiss seemed to hold all the cards."

Team Up with the BATNAs Themselves!

A classic example of this is "club deals," which have been a hot topic in investment circles. Club deals are where several investment firms will bid for an acquisition target together rather than against each other. This certainly eliminates some of the BATNA for the seller. To counter such moves, some sellers—like GE, which was shopping around to sell its plastics division for US$10 billion or so a while back—would announce they would not sell to a club deal. It should be noted that in some countries club deals may violate antitrust regulations. I am not advocating club deals here. I am just using them as an example.

Because BATNA is so important in determining the size of the win, and there are so many ways to change the BATNA, it is critical to invest time and resources in understanding the issues. As Tom Peters, a best-selling author seen by many as a management guru, advises, "She (he) who is best prepared wins! Out-study, out-read, out-research the competition" and "Know more (lots more!) than the person on the other side of the table."[4]

REFRAME

A young man asked a priest, "May I smoke while I pray? The priest answered angrily, "Certainly not." Another young man asked the same priest: "May I pray while I smoke?" The priest answered, "Good child."

Another story—as Professor Deepak Malhotra of HBS tells it— when President Theodore Roosevelt of the United States was campaigning for reelection in 1912, his campaign office made a brochure. The brochure included a picture of the president, together with information on his campaign. Three million copies were made, but only days before the brochures were supposed to be distributed, the campaign office realized they did not have the rights to use the picture. The rights belonged to a privately owned studio (call it Studio X). There was not enough time for a reprint.

The first reaction to solving the problem would be to send a representative to negotiate with Studio X as soon as possible. But this approach could have cost millions as copyright law allowed the copyright owner to demand up to a dollar a copy. What did the campaign office do? They sent a telegram to Studio X with the following content: PLANNING TO PRINT 3 MILLION COPIES OF CAMPAIGN SPEECH WITH YOUR PHOTOGRAPH. HOW MUCH ARE YOU WILLING TO PAY FOR OPPORTUNITY? Studio X quickly responded: APPRECIATE OPPORTUNITY, BUT CAN ONLY AFFORD $250. The campaign team accepted graciously.

These two stories illustrate the power of reframing (a concept also referred to as *framing*): gaining an advantage by changing the perception of a situation. Reframing is especially powerful if you can reframe to appeal to the interests of the other side of the negotiation. There are two ways to reframe: change the context of the situation or change the meaning of the situation. "Context reframing" means taking the same behavior, experience, or event but seeing it in a different context. The story about smoking and praying is context reframing. The behavior, praying and smoking at the same time, remains unchanged. What is changed is the context of the behavior— whether it takes place when one is smoking or when one is praying.

The story about President Roosevelt's brochure has an element of "meaning reframing." Meaning reframing is taking the same situation and context but changing what it means. The situation in the Roosevelt case is that the campaign wanted to use the picture from Studio X. The situation could be interpreted to have two very different meanings for Studio X. One meaning was this was another customer that wanted to use its picture. So the natural reaction would be to charge the campaign office. But the campaign office got Studio X to interpret the situation differently. Instead of "just another customer," it was a privilege and a marketing opportunity for the studio. So the natural arrangement would be to ask studios to bid for the privilege. This is content reframing.

LISTEN

Listening helps in the gathering of critical information like real interests and BATNA. It also makes the other side feel that they are heard and understood, helping you develop a positive relationship and an atmosphere conducive to discussion. This is not too different from what they teach in marriage counseling and parenting. In fact, I remember from one of my HBS classes that one of the most powerful strategic moves in a negotiation is to show the other side that you are listening, hearing, and understanding. This is applicable to both your personal and your professional life. However, it must be noted that hearing and understanding do not mean agreeing. In fact, they often provide ammunition for you to disagree later because you understand the other side's argument well enough for an effective rebuttal. This observation was a revelation to many HBS students, who tend to be accustomed to doing most of the talking rather than listening.

To make the other side feel heard and understood, these are the key techniques:

- Focus on listening.
- Paraphrase what you have heard in a positive, nonthreatening way.
- Ask questions that help the other side clarify their points.

Focus on Listening

Do not try to work on counterarguments in your head while the other side is talking, even if the speaker is repetitive, illogical, and long-winded.

Paraphrase

Retell what you have heard in a positive, nonthreatening way. Some key phrases:

"I can understand where you are coming from. Let me try to explain it to make sure I am not making any mistake . . ."
"I think what you are saying is . . . am I right?"
"I can see your point. You mean . . . Is my understanding correct?"

When you paraphrase in a positive way, the other side feels heard and understood.

Ask Questions

Help the other side clarify their points. This way, they feel you really want to understand what they say. Sometimes when you ask these questions, the other side can see the weakness of their own arguments. Questions must be asked tactfully, framed in terms such as these:

> "I got a little confused by that point. Do you mind elaborating?"
> "If I understand you correctly, you mean xxx. But what do you think about yyy?"

BUILD A GOLDEN BRIDGE

"Building a golden bridge" is another key concept taught in HBS negotiation classes. It means giving a face-saving way for the other party to concede or to agree. This concept of face-saving is well explained in the book *Getting to Yes* by Professor Roger Fisher from Harvard Law School and Professor William Ury from Harvard Business School, both very much involved in the negotiation projects and programs at Harvard:

> In English, "face-saving" carries a derogatory flavor. People say, "We are doing that just to let them save face" implying that a little pretense has been created to allow someone to go along without feeling bad. The tone implies ridicule.
>
> This is a grave misunderstanding of the role and importance of face-saving. Face-saving reflects a person's need to reconcile the stand he takes in a negotiation or an agreement with his principles and with his past words and deeds (this reconciliation is the "golden bridge"). . . .
>
> Often in a negotiation people will continue to hold out not because the proposal on the table is inherently unacceptable, but simply because they want to avoid the feeling or the appearance of backing down to the other side. If the substance can be phrased or conceptualized differently so that it seems a fair outcome, they will then accept it. . . . (The importance of face-saving) should not be underestimated.[5]

Herb Cohen, negotiation consultant to some of the largest corporations and government agencies in North America, who has also taught at Harvard University, wrote about the same idea in *You Can Negotiate Anything*:

Face is who I want the others to think I am. It is how a person wants to be seen publicly. When I am concerned with my saving face after a difficult negotiation, I want to make sure that the stature I have always projected in terms of prestige, worth, dignity, and respect will not be diminished. . . .

You must always keep in mind the physical law that "for every action there is a reaction." The gist of this was verbalized by Bernard Baruch when he said "Two things are bad for the heart—running up stairs and running down people."[6]

It is important to "save face" for the other party. So build a golden bridge. Make sure there is a face-saving way for the other side to agree with your proposal. Roger Fisher and William Ury gave this example of face saving: a major city government and its Hispanic community made an agreement on municipal jobs for this minority community. But the mayor refused to endorse the agreement. This was because he was not involved in the negotiation and he felt he would lose face. In the end, the only way for the terms of this agreement to be implemented was for the agreement to be withdrawn, allowing the mayor to announce the exact same terms as his own initiative. He got his "face."[7]

Notes

1. Pankaj Ghemawat, *British Satellite Broadcasting Versus Sky Television* (Boston: Harvard Business School Press, 1993).
2. Michael D. Watkins and Sarah G. Matthews, "Strategic Deal-Making at Millennium Pharmaceuticals," *Harvard Business Review* (September 1999), available for purchase online at www.harvardbusiness.org (access date: January 25, 2009).
3. David A. Lax and James K. Sebenius, "3-D Negotiation: Playing the Whole Game," *Harvard Business Review* (November 2003) 65–74; available for purchase online at www.harvardbusiness.org (access date: January 25, 2009).
4. Tom Peters, "Getting Things Done: The P&I 34", available online: www.tompeters.com/slides/uploaded/PandI34_091604.ppt, slide 9 (access date: January 14, 2009).
5. Roger Fisher and William Ury, *Getting to Yes* (New York: Penguin Group, 1992), 28–29.
6. Herb Cohen, *You Can Negotiate Anything*, (New York: Bantam Books, 1982), 189–191.
7. Roger Fisher and William Ury, *Getting to Yes*, (New York:, Penguin Group, 1992), 29.

3

SPEAK SO PEOPLE WILL

LISTEN

"A" FOR ARTICULATE

HBS is well-known for its "case teaching" method. The classes are almost never in lecture format. Instead, students are given cases to read before each class. (See the sidebar for explanation of what a case is.) During class, the professor will use questions to lead a group of 80 people into discussions of the case. You may be called on by the professor or you may raise your hand to volunteer to tell the class your views. Usually, over 50 percent of your grade is based on such class discussion participation. Therefore, you must work very hard to get the opportunity to speak—and when you get airtime, you must speak very well to have any chance of getting the top grade.

What Is an HBS Case?

HBS has an official explanation of what a case is and how it is taught:

"Typically, an HBS case is a detailed account of a real-life business situation, describing the dilemma of the 'protagonist'—a real person with a real job who is confronted with a real problem. Faculty and their research assistants spend weeks at the company that is the subject of the case. The resulting case presents the story exactly as the protagonist saw it, including ambiguous evidence, shifting variables, imperfect knowledge, no obvious right answers, and a ticking clock that impatiently demands action. Though every case is different, nearly all center on one overarching question: *What should the protagonist do?* In their two years at HBS, students study more than 500 cases—500 chances to join their classmates to test themselves against the rock-hard realities of life in business."[1]

HBS is extremely competitive. When you get to speak, you will only have about a minute or two before other people will try to interrupt you with their viewpoints. At least 40 hands will be raised as soon as people think they can attack your point or when they think they have a better point (if you are simply a boring speaker) or even when you are still in the middle of your speech. Whatever point you make, you must also be prepared to think on your feet to defend your views when you are challenged by the professor or your classmates. I have had classes when a student had to go on the defensive against the professor and 79 other students!

You discuss two to three cases, each for an hour to two, every day for two years. People, especially professors, often joke that HBS has such a system so that professors do not have to prepare for class since there is no lecture. Also, professors are never wrong in such a system, as they only facilitate class discussions and never have to lecture on their own views. In reality what the case teaching method highlights is that most business situations have no obvious right or wrong answer. The key skill is to be able to analyze and evaluate the situation and the options. Most importantly, you must be able to articulate and defend your analysis and your views intelligently and succinctly; and you must be good on your feet.

In business, you need to be articulate to get a good job, attract investors, motivate your staff, negotiate with your suppliers, and sell to your customers. Ability to speak in a logical, persuasive, and confident manner is invaluable. "Brilliant but inarticulate" may be a description that would apply to a nuclear scientist but not to any of the head honcho business types we see in business school. They are all brilliant *and* articulate. If they are not articulate when they enter HBS, they will be when they graduate.

I have found three techniques particularly useful in helping me articulate logically, persuasively, and confidently: structured logic, storytelling, and detailed practice.

Structured Logic

This technique involves using logic to structure facts and data to make a point. Structured logic helps both you and the audience. It helps you because it forces you to think clearly and logically. It ensures your point makes sense. It helps the audience because it is easy to follow and understand.

Structured logic comes in two types, deductive and inductive. Deductive logic looks like this:

A = B, B = C, therefore A = C. "A = C" is the "so what," the logical conclusion.

Inductive logic looks like this:

A, B, and C lead to D as the "so what" or conclusion. A, B, and C are "parallel," which means they are different arguments supporting D and they do not bear a cause-and-effect relationship with each other.

Thinking and speaking (and writing) in bullet points is often very helpful in organizing data into logic. The bullet points should either be deductive or inductive. For example:

- I like gentle and clean cats.
- Milo is a cat.
- Milo is also gentle and clean.
- → Therefore, I like Milo.

Here, the point is deduced from the data and facts.

Alternatively, I could argue that I like Milo (the point induced from the list of data and facts) because:

- He is fond of me.
- He is gentle.
- He is clean.
- He is a cat.

People who speak well often have very tight logic. Tight logic means three things. First, the data and facts should clearly support the argument. Second, any given argument is either deductive or inductive and not a mix of the two. The following is an example of loose and relatively ineffective logic:

I like Milo because:

- He is gentle (inductive).
- His fur is an ugly grayish color (unclear how this supports "I like Milo").

- I will be very sad when he dies one day (logic changed from inductive in first bullet point to deductive).

Third, for a single argument, it is usually more effective to have only three to five bullet points than to have a long laundry list. In the HBS classroom, you have no other choice. Each time you speak, the professor and your fellow classmates usually have patience for only one or two arguments, each supported by one or two (at most three) bullet points. It is not uncommon for a long deductive argument to get cut off by the professor's, "Where is this argument going? What is your point?" (A similarly long inductive argument is apt to get cut off with: "You have made your point. Let's move on to someone else.")

In consulting, we have a "rule of three." This rule of thumb is to have three bullet points for each argument, for a number of reasons. Too many bullet points can confuse and overwhelm the audience. It is generally believed that people tend to remember at most three things, not more. With too many bullet points, I usually find it possible to group some of them together or to eliminate some of the less important ones. Fewer than three bullet points will make it seem that the supporting data is rather thin. Of course, three is only a rule of thumb. It is not uncommon to have a range of two to five.

Structured logic can be used to make a simple, single argument, but it can also be used to organize more complex arguments. In the following example, a more complex argument, the central question is "How many favorite pets do I have?" There are five levels of argument, distinguished by Roman numerals, indentation, and bullets.

I have three favorite pets ("so what" or conclusion induced from below)	I
(i) Milo the cat. I like Milo because ("so what" or conclusion induced):	II
• he is fond of me. I know this because ("so what" induced)	III
– he kisses me whenever he sees me	IV
– he does not let anyone hug him except me	IV
– he runs away whenever my mother and dad try hug him	V
– he screamed last time my school friends tried to hug him	V
– he scratched the postman who tried to hug him	V
– he purrs whenever I call his name	IV
• he is gentle	III
• he is clean	III

(ii) Kilo the dog. I like Kilo because ("so what" deduced):   II
- my father bought Kilo for me   III
- I like everything my father bought me   III
- So I like Kilo   II

(iii) Silo the fish (and so on through the argument.)   II

Storytelling

I have been taught two types of storytelling. While they look mutually exclusive, they are actually complementary. I will first explain each of them and then how they can be interwoven.

The first type is what I term "factual storytelling." It was taught to me in my consulting days and what I typically use in my presentations. Basically, it just means using structured logic to solve whatever strategic, investment, or operational issue I was given. It is similar to the previous five-level example of pet preferences, except for having more levels with more complex quantitative and qualitative analyses and arguments.

The second type, I first learned when I was involved in a media start-up in 1999 and 2000. I was the chief executive officer. My chief operating officer was a retired movie director. I was preparing a presentation to potential investors. I rehearsed it in front of him and a few of my key managers. My COO dozed off after the first half of my slides. I did not mind as he was in the company because of his creative mind, not for his business sense. At the end of the rehearsal, I asked everyone for their comments. The COO woke up and commented, "It is so boring. Why don't you tell a story?" I said, "But this is a story." He answered, "This is not a story."

I did not think much about that incident until I was interviewing to hire a new sales manager. The interviewee was a lady whose résumé was only marginal. I had my usual list of questions. I asked her to describe her latest achievements. Instead of giving me a list such as the number of new clients she signed or the number of staff people she oversaw, she told me,

My last company was almost in bankruptcy. The sales manager and assistant manager both left for better opportunities. The CEO was so busy fighting off bankers and creditors that he had no time to organize the remaining, totally demoralized sales force. I was the only experienced person left. The other four left on the team were all young and inexperienced. I could have found another job but I did not want to leave the rest of the team behind. The company would definitely fall apart very quickly with no sales team and everyone would lose their jobs very soon. So I stayed on and worked hard. We worked out a strategy of focusing on the long-term clients as the sales cycle would be shorter. The company declared bankruptcy last month. But I felt I tried my best. My CEO thanked me in tears when he gave me my severance check.

I was very moved by the story. First, it was more interesting and engaging than the typical self-touting laundry lists most interviewees would give. Second, the story, if really true, told me a lot about this person—she is loyal to her company, considerate to her staff and colleagues, and able to handle a crisis. The image of the CEO in tears handing her the check was vivid. I did not hire her in the end because there were other people more qualified, but she definitely left a strong impression. She was bottom of my list before the interview but within the top five after.

I did not put the COO incident and the memorable interview together until I read a *Harvard Business Review* article a year or two later. The article, titled "Storytelling That Moves People—A Conversation with Screenwriting Coach Robert McKee," has the following introduction in bold print:

"Forget about PowerPoint and statistics. To involve people at the deepest level, you need stories. Hollywood's top writing consultant reveals the secrets of telling them."[2]

In the article, McKee explains, "I know the storytelling method works, because after I consulted with a dozen corporations whose principals told exciting stories to Wall Street, they all got their money."[3]

After I read the article, I had a revelation. This is another kind of storytelling. In my mind, I call it "emotional storytelling." It is not just factual. It is like anecdotes but used in a more extensive, organized, purposeful, and dramatic way. I did more research to understand its key success factors. I found that a good emotional story in business has a lot of similarities with the kind of age-old classics like "Beauty and the Beast" or "Cinderella" that we tell our children and that they love listening to over and over again:

A beginning tailored to entice the audience. "Once upon a time in a faraway place lived a beautiful young lady" attracts the attention and imagination of young children. In the same way, the most powerful emotional business storytelling deliberately starts with a beginning that catches attention of the target audience, such as "my last company was almost in bankruptcy" to an interviewer or "either we change the way we do business or we may as well fold the company today" to a group of executives. Great stories start with a dramatic momentum that can be built on rather than with unnecessary and boring details. For example, "Cinderella" does not start with how Cinderella's father chose his new wife and the interviewee did not start with what the company did or how she first joined it.

An engaging and exciting middle. Great fairytales are full of suspense and emotional ups and downs, with the hero or heroine fighting and then overcoming antagonists and obstacles. The bigger the difficulties and the greater the suspense, the more interesting the story. Cinderella had no clothes, no carriage, and a rigid deadline. She had lost her shoe. Cinderella was sad, then happy because of the fairy Godmother, then scared again when the clock struck 12. The interviewee faced an employer going bankrupt, saw her superiors resign, and was left with a weak team. Both of these examples have a central character: Cinderella and the interviewee. Audiences generally identify more with people and characters in the stories than with abstract discussion.[4] When there is no one central character, characters can be woven into the body of the story. For example: "In the next 10 minutes, I will show you five reasons why our business will disappear within five years if we continue with business as usual." Then, one reason could include the story of how a big customer was disappointed and another reason could include the story of how a group of salesmen felt helpless.

A strong conclusion that drives the message home. When the audience realizes that the story is about to finish, their attention generally goes up. Fairytales usually end with a glamorous, happy ending with the good getting rewarded and the evil defeated: "And the Prince and Cinderella lived happily ever after" while the evil stepmother and stepsisters were left to gnash their teeth in frustration. In business, stories should end with a purpose, such as reinforcing a message or defining the course of action against current challenges. The ending should tie the story up "without wandering, but without being too abrupt . . . (and not) merely summarize what you've said so far."[5] The interview example demonstrated an effective ending: "My CEO thanked me in tears when he gave me my severance check." It brought the story to an end concisely and smoothly, reinforcing the message that she had made sacrifices for her last company that would make any boss thankful.

The two kinds of storytelling, rational and emotional, actually reinforce each other. An emotional story with no facts will not be credible, and will not drive any significant business decisions and actions. On the other hand, a factual story with no emotion can be dry (see how my COO fell asleep), easy to forget, and weak in creating a deep buy-in in the audience, as explained by sociologist Andrew Greeley: "(Emotional) storytelling is so powerful because it short-circuits dull, factual discourse. Storytelling makes a leap from the imagination of the storyteller to the imagination of the listener, from the memory of the presenter to the memory of the hearer, from his life to the lives of his audience, from his stories to their stories."[6]

Therefore, nowadays, I always try to combine the two. I will weave emotional stories into factual stories. I will also try to weave facts into emotional stories.

Detailed Practice

I once had coffee with my favorite professor at HBS. I told him, "I really enjoy your class. The discussions are always guided to review the key learnings with a 'wow' effect. Your jokes are always funny, insightful, and memorable." He answered, "Thank you. I practice hard, especially my jokes." I thought this was another one of his jokes. But I later learned that he was serious.

It was a relief for me to find out that even speaking gurus practice and rehearse to ensure smooth delivery of their lectures, presentations, or key arguments. I have made a good number of presentations and boardroom arguments in my career. I would consider myself an experienced speaker. But I am still obsessive in my practice. I rehearse aloud as if I am really making the presentations. This helps make sure I know each word I am going to say. I practice where I would pause. I practice jokes so they are inserted appropriately with the punch line delivered at the right time. Last time I made a 10-minute presentation to a client's board of directors, I spent more than two hours just practicing aloud. I even practice aloud before important phone calls, rehearsing how to open, deliver, and close the conversations.

Before I finish this chapter, a small digression on two points I learned not from HBS but from having spent years working for a U.S. consulting firm and working with native English-speaking clients:

Non-native English accent—get rid of it. When I first joined the consulting firm about 10 years ago, I had a hard time getting to work on good projects. So after a few months, I went to talk to the vice president in charge of staffing. I still remember his exact words. "Maybe it's your accent. You know you do not speak like an American. You have that British plus California plus Chinese accent." I was shocked. I never even knew accent was an issue. I had top grades at Stanford and had many American friends. I interviewed and got all the job offers I wanted. Nobody ever told me about an accent problem. I went back and told some of my fellow junior colleagues. They were all appalled (or at least appeared appalled) by this borderline racial discrimination incident. One of them told me I should file a formal complaint with senior management. I did not launch the complaint, but I became much more conscious in trying to speak like an American. It was hard work, as accent is an ingrained habit. It takes much time and effort to change. Also even different parts of the United States have different accents. New York English sounds slightly different from Boston English, which sounds different from Los Angeles English.

Over the years, I have seen many cases of discrimination against people who do not speak with a perfect native accent. Even though few people would ever admit they discriminate against non-native English speakers and most know very well a non-native accent has nothing to do with intelligence, unspoken discrimination does exist. You can go to Amazon.com and find many books documenting such discrimination. Therefore, if possible, when you train yourself to speak well and you know you may have to deal with native English speakers, try to work on your accent. There are books you can read and tutorials you can attend. I also urge parents to expose their children to native English at a young age. The older a person is, the more difficult it is to change an accent.

Non-English languages—the more the merrier. I speak only English, Mandarin, and Cantonese. This is one of my biggest regrets in life. My son, who is only four years old, has been trained in seven languages. I believe, if possible, it is always good to learn many languages. First, people, especially in the United States (HBS included) and Asia, tend to have immediate respect for those who can speak many languages. Second, languages can open doors to many career options: diplomatic, high fashion (French), video game animation (Japanese), and many others.

This is a real-life story: I know a man who worked for a Fortune 100 company in its U.S. headquarters. He was an average middle manager. Then one day, he was called to a meeting with an executive several levels his superior. He was told the company was about to sign a major joint venture in Japan and they needed a representative in Japan to ensure communication with the partner. He was chosen because he was the only one in the firm who could speak Japanese. Things happened very fast after that. He ended up with a major promotion, an enviable expatriate package, and an important job. This is more or less because he was the only one in the company who could speak Japanese. This example is always on my mind when I mentor young people to learn as many languages as they can. I also advise parents to expose their children to many languages before the age of six. Research has shown that children can learn languages very easily without an accent then, and find it much harder later.

A Picture Is Worth a Thousand Words

Visual aids are important tools for rational storytelling. And even though visual aids can be product samples, mockups, three-dimensional models, and video, the most common type still seems to be PowerPoint slides.

With the case study method, neither professors nor students have to make many full PowerPoint presentations at HBS.[7] Therefore, the skills I have are from my consulting days. I have used these skills a few times at HBS, once for a full presentation and occasionally for presenting supporting evidence for my class comments. Some of my HBS friends have found the skills useful. Therefore, even though I did not learn these skills from HBS, I thought it would be useful to discuss them here.

Three key skills go into making effective PowerPoint slides:

- Organizing individual slides into a smoothly flowing presentation that the audience can easily follow
- Designing individual data slides
- Designing individual text slides

Flow

One easy and effective way to organize the slides is to follow structured logic. Using the example "I have three favorite pets" from the "Structured Logic" section of this chapter, the first slide would look like Figure 3.1.

Sometimes, you may put some overview slides like a table of contents or discussion of the context up front. But this slide is the first "content" slide. With this slide, you have established the structure of your presentation. It is clear where you are going.

The rest of the presentation flows from this first slide. Each of the points on the first slide becomes a section of the presentation. For example, the first section to follow will be on Milo, possibly with the next slide looking like the one shown in Figure 3.2.

Figure 3.1 PowerPoint Introduction Slide

I HAVE THREE FAVORITE PETS

Milo the cat
Kilo the dog
Silo the fish

Figure 3.2   PowerPoint Section Slide

FIRST FAVORITE: MILO THE CAT

Milo is my favorite because:
- He is fond of me
- He is gentle
- He is clean

Each of these points, in turn, becomes a data slide, a word slide, or a subsection. For example, see Figure 3.3.

For longer presentations or presentations with more complex logic, it is often useful to put icons in the top left or top right corner of each slide to help the audience follow the flow. For example, see Figure 3.4.

In these figures, the first slide is the conclusion of the whole presentation. The first slide of the first section is the conclusion for that section. Unless there is a reason why the audience has to be kept in suspense, I usually prefer to start business presentations with the conclusions. Whether people agree with the conclusion or not, declaring the conclusion up front helps the audience understand and follow the structured logic. It is also easier in

Figure 3.3   PowerPoint Subsection Slide

MILO IS FOND OF ME

I know Milo is fond of me because:
- He kisses me whenever he sees me
- He does not let anyone hug him except me
  - he runs away whenever my mother and dad try to hug him
  - he screamed last time my school friends tried to hug him
  - he scratched the postman who tried to hug him
- He purrs whenever I call his name

Figure 3.4   PowerPoint Introduction Slide with Orientation Block

---

FIRST FAVORITE: MILO THE CAT

| Milo |
| Kilo |
| Silo |

Milo is my favorite because:
- He is fond of me
- He is gentle
- He is clean

---

case the presentation has to be cut short or rushed as a result of digressions or emergencies. Even when the structured logic is deductive, I will still show the conclusion first and then the logic leading to the conclusion.

Data Slides

There are two major types of slides: text slides and data slides (which feature little or no text). The key to a data slide is the art of using the most appropriate charts or graphs to analyze and display data. All standard graphs and charts, such as scatter, bar, stacked bar, and so on, can be useful depending on the data and analysis. Instead of going through a laundry list of basic charts, here are four of the nonstandard ones that I have found most useful in my career for generating insightful analysis and impressive visual aids:

- Matrix
- Moon chart
- Cascading chart
- Area chart

Two-by-Two Matrix

A matrix is a powerful analytical tool and visual aid. Especially at the two-by-two level, which is the most common choice, it is simple yet very effective. It can be applied whenever the outcome of a certain issue depends on two critical factors or drivers, with each of them having two key options, categories, sets of outcomes, parameters, or whatever.

Example One: Figure 2.1 sets out the basics of the interests involved in the Sky/BSB negotiation for control of British satellite television, where the financial consequences depended on the decision by Sky and BSB. Each company had binary options: fight or exit. Hence a 2×2 matrix is an effective way for analyzing and displaying the situation.

Example Two: Perhaps one of the best-known two-by-two matrices is the growth-share matrix first published by Bruce Henderson, founder of BCG, in the 1970s. The matrix is still widely described in business books and taught in business schools. Though it was not explicitly taught at HBS, it was referred to in many discussions. However, it must be noted that its application to today's business could be tricky and sometimes subject to debate beyond the scope of this book. I include it here as a classic example of the two-by-two format rather than as a business concept.

Figure 3.5 Henderson Growth-Share Matrix

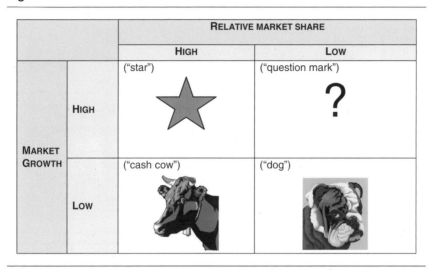

The matrix was first intended to be used by multi-business corporations to view their portfolio. The matrix says that free cash flow of a business is driven by two key factors: market growth and relative market share of the business.[8] Conceptually, it looks like Figure 3.5.

If a business has high relative market share in a low-growth market, it is expected to be a "cash cow" because it generates cash in excess of what is needed to maintain market share. If a business has high market share in a high-growth market, it is a "star" because even though it will require cash to sustain its growth, it will eventually become a cash cow when growth stabilizes. Low share and low growth indicates a "dog"—a poor prospect—as cash generated is more than used up to maintain share. Lastly, low share, high growth is a question mark as it can become star, cow, or dog.

Figure 3.6 illustrates the matrix with data.

To make this scatter graph into a two-by-two matrix, the graph needs to be divided into four quadrants by adding two lines: a horizontal line dividing high growth from low and a vertical line dividing high share from low. This can be tricky and depends on factors including industries, geographies, company situation, and judgment, all of which affect cash generated and cash needed for reinvestment. However, as a rule of thumb, a relative market share of 2x is considered high and stable (at least for fast-moving consumer goods) and a market growth of 10 percent or above is generally considered high.

Figure 3.6 Data for a Growth-Share Matrix

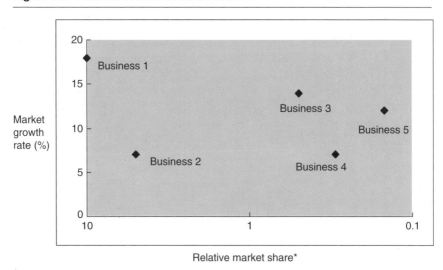

Relative market share*

---

* Relative market share is drawn on log rather than linear scale so that equal distances represent an equal percentage increase (for example, the distance between 10x and 1x is the same as the distance between 1x and 0.1). It addition, the smaller numbers can be displayed clearly.

It is often useful to add a third dimension to scatter graphs. The size of each data point on the graph can be drawn to scale relative to the importance of that point. For growth-share matrix, this is often the revenue size, as shown in Figure 3.7.

I have found that this added dimension is useful not just for two-by-two matrices but also for scatter graphs in general. Knowing the relative importance of the different data points helps you prioritize and make decisions. In addition to revenue size, net profit size or contributions or other relevant quantities can also be used. The choice depends on what data you can get, and of that range of figures, what best indicates importance. However, it must be noted that it is the area of the circle, not the radius or diameter, that should be drawn to scale to for the measure in question. This is because the circle area gives the visual impact of the relative size of the various data points. Using radius or diameter will greatly exaggerate differences.

Example Three: This third example is described in detail in Appendix A of this book. It is a two-by-two matrix I designed for a client to monitor the success (and failure) of tenants in the shopping mall properties of a company. It turns out that retail tenant success is driven by sales per square foot of store

Figure 3.7   Three-Dimensional Matrix

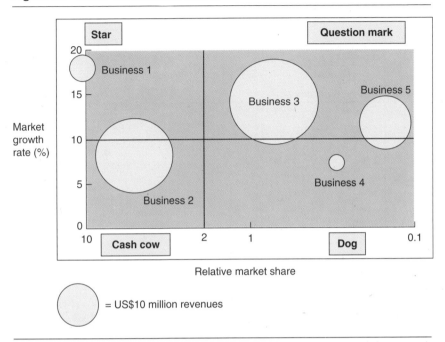

space and the rent the store owner pays as a percentage of monthly sales. The higher the former and the lower the latter, the more successful the tenant is, as shown in Figure 3.8.

I use this as a third example because it demonstrates how the two dividing lines, vertical and horizontal, can be drawn based on company and industry characteristics as well as creativity. I used dots instead of drawn-to-scale circles here because the intended user seemed likely to find the additional dimension (circle size) too complicated. Also, the tenants tracked on the matrix were very similar in size.

Example Four: Beyond two-by-two, you can have two-by-three or three-by-two or three-by-three matrices and so on. As an example, Figure 3.9 shows one of the best-known three-by-three matrices, the industry attractiveness-business strength matrix developed jointly by General Electric and McKinsey and Company back in the 1970s and early 1980s.

Again, I use this example here not to explain how to apply this specific theory but to illustrate how three-by-three matrices can be used. But three is about the limit. People do sometimes use four-by-four or even larger matrices, but I find such matrices too complicated. You will usually have

Figure 3.8   Setting the Matrix Dividers

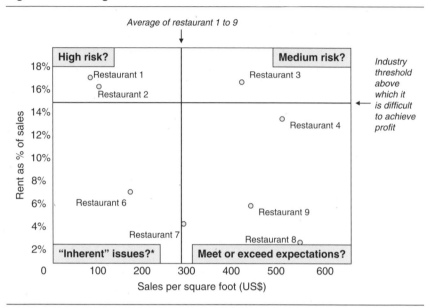

Average of restaurant 1 to 9

* These have low sales but rent is still quite low for the tenant's overall financials. The tenant has healthy financials but may not be maximizing the sales (hence rental) potential of the space it is occupying. Therefore, it is important to understand the reasons behind its place on the chart.

Figure 3.9   Three-by-Three Matrix*

		INDUSTRY ATTRACTIVENESS		
		HIGH	MEDIUM	LOW
BUSINESS STRENGTH	HIGH	Investment and growth	Selective growth	Selectivity
	MEDIUM	Selective growth	Selectivity	Harvest (divest)
	LOW	Selectivity	Harvest (divest)	Harvest (divest)

* Placement of businesses within the matrix provides an analytic map for managing them. For businesses above the diagonal, a company may consider pursuing strategies of investment and growth; those along the diagonal may be considered for selective investment; those below the diagonal may be best sold, liquidated, or run purely for cash.

better ways to analyze and display the issue when a large matrix suggests itself.

The key here is practice. Next time you are trying to solve a complicated issue or writing a presentation to articulate your thoughts, I strongly encourage you to consider putting the ideas in a matrix. Even if eventually you find that it does not apply well, the practice will help you master this versatile tool.

Moon Chart

Moon charts are useful when you have a list of items and need to rank them. For examples, see Figures 3.10 and 3.11.

The moons are circles that are shaded differently to symbolize different rankings. The examples show two of the possible applications of moon charts:

- When an "item" needs to be assessed. In Figure 3.10, the item is a slide. The item can also be a product, a service, an acquisition target, an industry, a staff member, an issue, or any other thing you can clearly define. To ensure a systematic and credible assessment, a list of criteria is generated based on valid sources. The moon chart allows the list and ranking to be clearly displayed.

Figure 3.10 Moon Chart 1: Slide Evaluation Criteria

	Criteria for an effective PowerPoint slide based on interviews with PowerPoint experts	How well this slide fulfils the criterion
Most	1. Effective title	◐
	2. Concise text	◑
Importance based on expert interviews	3. Insightful graphics	◐
	4. Authoritative data source	◐
	5. Overall easy to understand	◑
least	Total average ranking	slightly above ◐

◑ Fully fulfills criterion

◐ Does not fulfill criterion

Source: Expert interviews.

Figure 3.11 Moon Chart 2: Customers' Purchasing Criteria

Key purchase criteria for washing machines	Importance based on consumer surveys
1. Well-known brand	◑
2. Length of free warranty	◑
3. Free delivery and installation services	◐
4. Free telephone hotline	◯

◑ Most important

◯ Unimportant

- When a list of factors needs to be credibly prioritized. In Figure 3.11, a list of possible consumer purchase criteria is prioritized by using consumer survey data to identify the ones that are most important.

Three points to note when using moon charts:

- It is advisable to organize the list in a logical order: descending order of importance, chronological order, or whatever seems appropriate. I have found this useful as a discipline to ensure better organization of any list, both for analysis and for presentation to audience.
- Some people may prefer to use numbers (1, 2, 3), check marks (such as √, √√, √√√) or other symbols instead of the moons. In general, I prefer using moons because I feel they have a strong visual impact. They are especially appropriate where rankings are somewhat subjective rather than hard data.

Sometimes in addition to full moon, half moon, and blank moon, charts can also have quarter moon and three-quarters moon when more rankings are necessary. When the full moon is defined as top ranking, the different shadings make it easy for the audience to see if top ranking is almost achieved (three-quarter shading) or not (no shading or one-quarter shading).

However, there are also times when other symbols are more appropriate. In Figure 3.11, if the consumer survey had asked the consumers to rank each criterion on a scale of 1 to 5, then it would be more appropriate to use 1 to 5 instead of moons on the "moon chart." Similarly, if you are presenting to an audience who is used to checks or certain symbols or who might find moons difficult to understand (an example could be factory workers in a developing country), then other symbols may be preferable to moons.

- When appropriate, a rough average can be estimated using the moons or other symbols. An average is useful in helping make an overall assessment or draw an overall conclusion. This is shown in Figure 3.10.

Cascading Chart

Figures 3.12 and 3.13 present two examples of cascading charts.

A cascading chart is useful in displaying how quantitative values such as revenues, costs, headcount, and the like sum up to a final number. It is especially useful if additions and subtractions are both involved. It is difficult to display such complexity with other forms of charts, such as pie charts or stacked bar charts.

Area Chart

An area chart is useful when you have three variables of interest, say, x, y, and x multiplied by y. Figure 3.14 presents an example.

In this example, the chart displays headcount and average cost per head by job category. Moreover, the chart also displays the total headcount cost of each job category, which is represented by the area of each box:

Figure 3.12 Cascading Chart 1: Project Cost

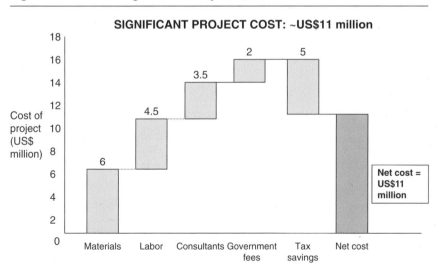

Figure 3.13 Cascading Chart 2: Project Profit

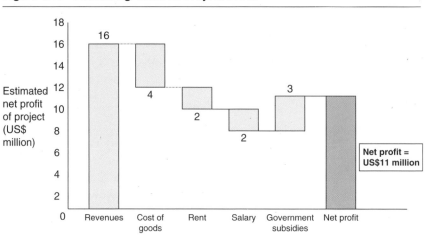

Area of each box = value on x-axis multiplied by value on y-axis
= headcount multiplied by average cost per head by category
= total headcount cost for each category

Hence by using this format instead of bar or scatter chart, you can show an additional third variable of interest to the analysis. In this example, it may

Figure 3.14 Area Chart

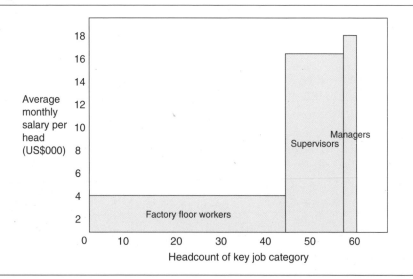

be important to know that while factory workers are the most numerous, their cost per head is so low that their total cost is smaller than that of the supervisors (can be seen by comparing the areas). Hence the organization may be described as "top heavy."

When using these four charts (and any other chart types) as visual aids and analytical tools, keep the following points in mind:

A chart is valuable only if it helps you make a point. It is sometimes tempting to show a chart where rare data could be displayed or where the data are so cleverly manipulated that the display would impress any intellectual. However, it is important to keep in mind that the chart is a means to an end. Any chart that does not help make your point is of no value and must not be included as a visual aid.

Each chart should be put on a PowerPoint slide with a title at the top and a data source at the bottom. In consulting, the rule is that the title should

- Be simple and concise, preferably eight words or fewer.
- Tell the audience the point of the chart, that is, the conclusion or the "so what" of the chart.

Novices are often tempted to use descriptive titles like "REVENUE CALCULATION" or "MARKET GROWTH" because those are easy to do. This is not "wrong"—but best practice is to use the title to tell the audience the "so what": why they are looking at the chart. This practice has two benefits. First, it forces a discipline on the author of the slide; you have to think through the "so what" of the chart and how the slide fits into the rest of the story. Second, it allows the audience a fast and simple way to understand the significance of the chart. Figure 3.12 also illustrates this kind of title.

Sometimes, the title cannot fully explain the point. This can be because the point is too complex. In such cases, a subtitle can be added below the title or a short text can be added to the bottom of the slide. Figures 3.15 and 3.16 show how to do this. It's best to stick to the title when feasible, because it is most direct. But these two techniques are available for use when necessary.

Putting the source on a slide is important for three reasons. The first is the credibility of the data. The second is just in case the audience asks in the middle of your presentation. The third is for future reference in case you or someone must find the data source at some future date. If raw data from the sources have been manipulated or adjusted, some people will put "analysis and estimates" after the list of sources to indicate this fact. Figure 3.16 also illustrates the use of a source note; it illustrates a complete slide with title and source. It should be noted that similar title and source rule applies to text slides.

Figure 3.15 Use of Subtitle

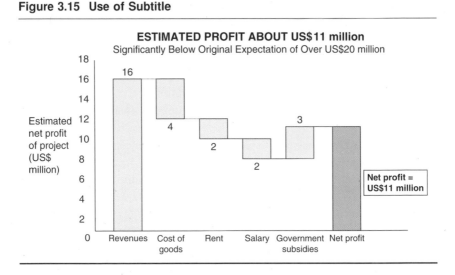

For important or complicated charts, it's usually best stick to the rule of one chart per slide. However, it may sometimes be necessary to put multiple charts on the same slide. This can be done as long as the charts all work to make a point simple enough for the audience to understand and absorb quickly and easily. Figure 3.17 is an example.

Figure 3.16 Use of Explanatory and Source Notes

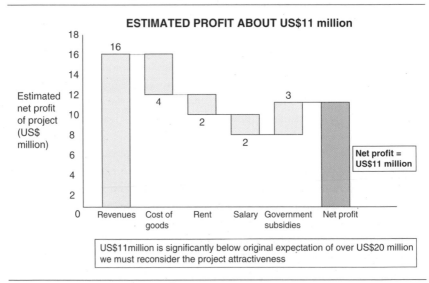

Source: Internal accounting data; analyst reports; analysis.

Figure 3.17 Multiple Charts on a Slide

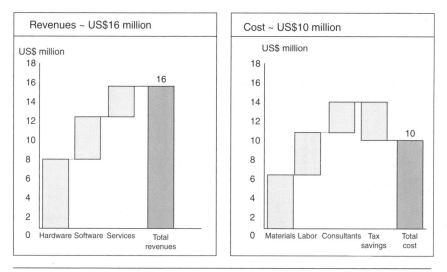

NET PROFIT APPREARS ATTRACTIVE ESTIMATED ~ US$6 million

Source: Internal accounting data; analyst reports; analysis.

The graph and chart examples I've presented so far are simply references. Visual aid design is often about creativity. The key is to know the point you want to make and then design an effective way to show the supporting data to make the point. Figure 3.18 is an example of a visual aid I have recently used that I have not used before. This is the foot traffic pattern for a grocery store. The data is collected by hiring part-time staff to stand at each aisle for two hours to record the actual traffic.

This chart looks somewhat messy and raw. But it is indeed an effective chart because the point is not to show the details but to show that certain sections have much heavier traffic than others.

Text Slides

For data graphs and charts, the format chosen is largely driven by the data and analysis needed. For text slides, however, the format is more a personal choice and personal style. My style is one of "less is more." This style fits me because the PowerPoint presentations I do are mostly visual aids to a verbal presentation rather than stand-alone documents. Therefore, it is not necessary to "cross all the *t*'s and dot all the *i*'s."

Figure 3.18   Hand-Drawn Traffic Pattern

MOST CUSTOMERS ONLY VISIT AISLES I TO IV

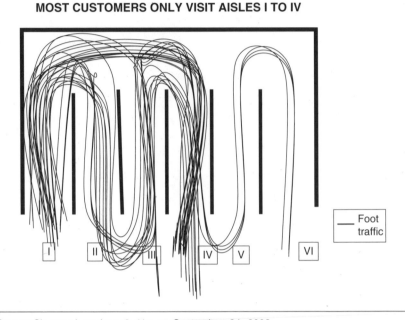

Source: Shopper interviews 9–11 a.m, September, 24 2008.

By "less is more," I mean:

First, minimize the number of text slides. I try to use pictures whenever possible. For example, Figure 3.19 shows a slide from my recent presentation to a client who was considering entering a new market. Instead of a narrative slide, I used a picture of a jigsaw puzzle.

Since there was no data or analysis involved, I could have used a simple text slide. But I decided to use a jigsaw picture for two reasons. First, it conveys the message that all four components are necessary and must work closely together. Second, it is visually more interesting and more memorable, especially important because the audience included sales managers and technical managers who could be overwhelmed by an overly analytical presentation. In general, whenever I have to write a text slide, the first thing I do is to think if I can draw a picture instead. If not, I go ahead and write the text. After I finish, I still keep looking at the text slide to see if I can put it into a picture.

If text is necessary, economize on the number of words on each text slide. I always use bullet points and subpoints. I find that in addition to

Figure 3.19   One Picture Equals

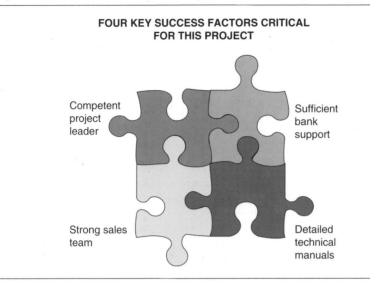

**FOUR KEY SUCCESS FACTORS CRITICAL
FOR THIS PROJECT**

Competent
project
leader

Sufficient
bank
support

Strong sales
team

Detailed
technical
manuals

helping enforce the discipline of structured logic, the natural breakdown provided by bullet points largely reduces the need for conjunctions and articles. Within each bullet point, I also spend a lot of time and effort to try to use the fewest number of words. For example, instead of "the project will be high in cost and low in risk," I may just write "high cost, low risk." Or instead of "we expect government to give us full support," I will write "expect full government support."

Remember to make bullet points under the same argument parallel, especially for inductive arguments. Parallel bullet points mean the bullet points have a similar, if not identical, grammatical structure. Figures 3.20 and 3.21 illustrate two types of parallel bullet points. In the first one, each bullet point starts with a verb. In the second, each starts with an adjective.

Figure 3.20   Parallel Construction: Verbs

BULLET POINTS ARE EFFECTIVE

Bullet points are effective because they can:
- Break a long argument into shorter, more easily understood points
- Reduce the use of conjunctions and articles
- Make inductive argument stand out

Figure 3.21   Parallel Construction: Adjectives

FOUR KEY SUCCESS FACTORS FOR PROJECT

To ensure success, four factors are essential:
- Competent team leader
- Strong sales team
- Sufficient bank support
- Detailed technical manuals

Making the bullet points parallel helps you make sure that the points are congruent with the logic. Parallel construction also makes it easier for the audience to understand and absorb the points.

WHEN YOU'RE IN A HOLE, STOP DIGGING

Training yourself to speak well also means knowing when it is time to say no more. There are at least two situations when it is better to shut up than to continue to speak, no matter how eloquent you are as a speaker:

Even people who are very good at speaking can find themselves saying the wrong thing. I still remember this scene. It was the first week of HBS, and one of my classmates was making a comment. He started well enough, but then his speech began to go wrong. Almost everyone in the class raised a hand to argue against him. Knowing something was not right, he started to "fine-tune" his point "I did not mean that. . . . What I meant was. . . . " But somehow the more he tried to talk himself out of it, the worse it became. Then the professor quietly walked up to him, looked him in the eye, and said to him in front of the class, "Rule #1 in speaking—when you are in a hole, stop digging." The whole class laughed, but this advice had so much truth that I remember it to this day.

Sometimes it is important to quit while you are ahead. In some situations, especially when your goal has already been achieved, the less you say, the less risk you have of saying something wrong. I learned this during my high school years, when history was my favorite subject, and I encountered the story of Kondraty Ryleyev. Ryleyev, a 19th-century Russian revolutionary, demanded modernization of the country. Eventually, he was arrested and sentenced to be hanged. On the day of the execution, as the trapdoor opened and Ryleyev dangled, the rope broke and he fell to the ground. At the time, such an event was seen as a sign from above to pardon the criminal. As Ryleyev stood up, he shouted out to the crowd something like this: "You see, in Russia they do not even know how to make rope!" The Tsar was almost signing the pardon when he heard what Ryleyev had said to the crowd. The Tsar was so infuriated that despite the general pardon rule, he decided to hang Ryleyev again the next day to "prove the contrary."

Notes

1. Discussion of case study available online: www.hbs.edu/mba/academics/howthe casemethodworks.html; access date: January 16, 2008.
2. Bronwyn Fryer, "Storytelling That Moves People: A Conversation with Screen-writing Coach Robert McKee," *Harvard Business Review* (June 2003); 81(6): 51–5, 136.
3. Bronwyn Fryer, "Storytelling That Moves People: A Conversation with Screen-writing Coach Robert McKee," *Harvard Business Review* (June 2003); 81(6): 51–5, 136.
4. Michael Hateetersley, "The Managerial Art of Telling a Story," *Harvard Management Update* (January 1997), No. U9701D.
5. Bronwyn Fryer, "Storytelling That Moves People: A Conversation with Screen-writing Coach Robert McKee," *Harvard Business Review* (June 2003); 81(6): 51–5, 136.
6. Andrew Greeley, *Furthermore* (New York: Forge Books, 2000).
7. This was true at least during my time there, 1997 to 1998. There have been some changes since then, and students may now be required to do more team projects, hence more presentations.
8. *Relative market share* is the company's market share relative to its biggest competitor. For example, if a company has 30 percent market share and its biggest competitor has the same, its relative market share is $1\times$. If the biggest competitor has 60 percent of market share, then the company's relative market share is $0.5\times$.

4

It's Who You Know

Why Network

To some extent, everyone knows the importance of networks, or *guanxi*. We all know from everyday experience that without knowing the right people, we may have a hard time getting a business permit, finding a client, making a sale, landing a job, and hiring the right employee. To say nothing of the personal stuff, like finding an ethical doctor, a competent lawyer, a piece of bargain property or a good nursery school for your kids. As Harvey Mackay (a popular speaker at many places including Harvard) says in his book *Dig Your Well Before You Are Thirsty*, "No matter how smart you are, no matter how talented, you can't do it alone."[1]

Besides anecdotal and everyday experience, a number of research studies conducted in the United States also confirm the importance of networks in business. In one study of 733 U.S. millionaires, nearly all the respondents (94 percent) rated "getting along with people (networking)" as either very important or important in accounting for their success. In the same survey, only 31 percent felt that "having a high IQ or superior intellect" was very important or important.[2]

For his classic 1974 "Getting a Job: A Study of Contacts and Careers," sociologist Mark Granovetter (a Harvard Ph.D.) interviewed several hundred professional and technical workers in the United States about how they found their current jobs.[3] Fifty-six percent of those he talked to found their jobs through a personal connection.

Networking is important not just for business. In their 1993 *Harvard Business Review* article "How Bell Labs Creates Star Performers," Robert Kelley and Judith Caplan wrote about the study they conducted of engineers at a major research laboratory to determine what attributes separated the 15–20 percent whom their peer group nominated as "stars" from the average performers.[4] One of the most important attributes was found to be "rapport with a network of key people." It was found that things went more smoothly for the stars because they put time into cultivating good relationships with people who could help them in their careers. This contradicts the general belief (especially as held by many parents) that scientific or academic superstars need only excel in their specialty and that networking is unimportant. In today's world, as Harvey Mackey notes, "Networking may not be rocket science, but studies prove it works for rocket scientists."[5] They need to network to:

- Know where research grants are available and who controls the money, so they can get a piece of the pie.
- Know how to get their achievements reported in the appropriate journals so they get the attention and profile they need.
- Know the latest developments in their fields so they can exploit any synergies possible.

In fact, many people state that the key reason to go to Harvard Business School is not to learn from the classes but to get into the network of HBS alumni. A 2007 report, "The Small World of Investing,"[6] studied 85 percent of the total assets under management in the United States from 1990 to 2006 and presented the following findings:

- Mutual fund managers invested more money in companies run by people they went to college or graduate school with than in companies where they had no such connections.
- Investments involving school ties, on average, did significantly better than those that did not. (One possible explanation for this is that fund managers knew more about their old schoolmates and hence could invest in the ones they knew were capable and competent.)
- The most common shared school in the study was found to be HBS.

Therefore, it is not surprising that many people go to HBS not for the classroom learning but for the networking. Networking includes not just people met while attending HBS but also the huge network of successful people who have attended or will attend the school and who appear at Harvard-organized or other events there. Personally, because of the alumni network, I have met with the president of Chanel, the head of the Economic Development Board in Singapore, the president of Tiffany's, the chairman of the Hong Kong Airport Authority, and other notables of business and government.[7]

WHO TO NETWORK WITH

The key to a successful network is variety and breath. In the job survey mentioned earlier, Granovetter found that of those who used a contact to find a job, less than 17 percent would describe that contact as a close friend. The rest would describe the contact more as an acquaintance.

Why is this? Granovetter believes that when it comes to finding out about new opportunities and information such as jobs, acquaintances (or "weak ties," as he calls them) are actually more important than close friends ("strong ties"). This is because your "strong ties" usually occupy pretty much the same world as you do. They most likely have a family and education background, social circle, profession, life experience, lifestyle, religion, and geographic location similar to yours. Therefore, you probably already know most of what they know. Your acquaintances, on the other hand, occupy different worlds. They are more likely to know something that you do not. Granovetter called this "the strength of weak ties." A broad network with many acquaintances hence represents a source of social power. The more acquaintances you have, the more powerful you are. Acquaintances give you access to opportunities and worlds you wouldn't otherwise have an easy way to reach.

HBS teaches you not to discriminate as you build your network. There are good reasons to avoid the assumption that a junior person is a meaningless person. After all, Bill Gates, one of the richest men in the world now, was a college dropout. Many successful people who came to speak at HBS had a modest family background, mediocre education, and have held some very junior positions early on in their career. Some have failed miserably in their early career, but all ended up wildly successful. Treating everybody with dignity and courtesy is not just good form. It is a good strategy.

Having variety and breadth does not mean you just aim to maximize the number of people in your network. You are not really acquainted unless the person remembers you and remembers something about you. The key is to be acquainted enough so the person can be counted on to remember you if you call or when appropriate occasions and opportunities arise.

The most successful networkers are referred to by some as "connectors."[8] The idea of connectors was most profoundly illustrated by an experiment that is very much related to the now well-known concept of "six degrees of separation." In the late 1960s, Harvard social psychologist Stanley Milgram did an experiment with a chain letter. He got the names of 160 people who lived in Omaha, a city in the U.S. Midwest, and mailed each of them a packet. Each packet had the name of the same stockbroker located near Boston, a city on the U.S. East Coast. The people were asked to write their name on the packet and then send it on to a contact they thought could get the packet to the stockbroker, or at least closer to the stockbroker. For example, the person might send it to a friend who lived in Boston or a friend in stock brokering near Massachusetts. The friend would be instructed to do the same until the packet arrived at the stockbroker. After the 160 packets reached the stockbroker, Milgram found that most of the packets reached the stockbroker after changing hands five or six times. This experiment is often quoted as one of the evidence of the concept of six degrees of separation—that everyone is linked to everyone else in six steps or less.

To me, the more important point demonstrated by Milgram's experiment is that of the six degrees of separation, some are much more important than the others. When Milgram analyzed the names on the packets, he found that the same three names appeared on half of the packets. These three people were the key to getting the packets to the stockbroker. Milgram's experiment tells that the six degrees of separation does not mean everyone is linked to everyone else in six random steps or less. The experiment says that a very small number of people, like these three, "know everyone"—and the rest of us are linked to the world through this small number of people.

These special few are the "connectors." Connectors make many friends because they see possibilities. While most people choose those they would like to know and often reject the people they do not think are "worth knowing," the connectors become acquainted with them all.

So the ideal is to become a connector. However, if you do not have the energy, social skills, or natural temperament to become a connector, the next best thing is get to know the connectors.

WHERE TO NETWORK

Since the idea is to have the broadest network possible, the key is to network wherever possible. School, friends' dinner parties, church, and special interest classes (yoga, Japanese, whatever interests you) are obvious and effective social places to meet people and build networks. When interviewed for this book, the connectors I know from HBS suggested two additional places: family friends and outgoing colleagues.

Many connectors I know from HBS recalled that the breadth of their networks got a kick start or a real boost through their family's connections. By their own initiative, at the urging of their parents, or just by chance, these people met up early in their career with a close family contact. Examples include the longtime family solicitor, a successful uncle, and their parents' best friend—someone close to the family personally or professionally, old, experienced in business, and possibly already a connector. It is effective, as Harvey Mackay explains,

> Why? Because most so-called gurus and old fuds like me are downright flattered when someone asks their opinion—on anything. . . .
> We have a network, and inevitably, it's going to evaporate. . . . Still, we like being a player, and one way to do that is to . . . offer a little godlike advice to whoever will listen.
> Make an appointment to see that "old friend of Dad's." Of course, you are not going to ask for a job, that would be too crude and obvious. . . . You want some career advice. Believe me, you'll get it. At length. . . . Once you've gotten it, that old family retainer will have an investment in your future. Your failure would reflect on them, on the quality of their advice, and on their continued relevance.[9]

Another obvious source of network members is your colleagues, including ex-colleagues. Your colleagues have friends and you can network with them too. Many people forget or underestimate the power of people who have recently left the company. Just because they have moved on (or been made to move on) is no reason to give up your relationships with them. In fact, there is a reasonably good chance they will become even more valuable members of your network. They will make new connections, which may well be connections you do not have. An example is an ex-colleague of mine who got fired because he was not performing well as a consultant. He was not good in analytics and he often made significant quantitative errors. Most people in the firm had little respect for his consulting abilities. Many people distanced themselves from him or made fun of him when he left. But he changed industries and went on to become a very senior executive at a major global manufacturing firm, where sales skills and market instinct proved much more important than analytics. Now most consulting firms are trying very hard to court him to become their client!

How to Network

In China, many people equate networking and *guanxi* with expensive gift-giving which is indeed one way to network, but it does not always work, and it is unlikely to as time goes on. As China develops, regulators will likely enact more effective anticorruption laws, and already gift-giving cannot be practiced in many developed countries. In addition, broad networks with many weak ties make expensive gifts impractical, and in any case a relationship that depends on gifts is fragile and unreliable—after all, someone else can always snatch the relationship by more expensive gifts.

To many at HBS, networking means getting to know people through conversations and communications. There are various degrees, from casual acquaintance to best friends. But the minimum threshold is that the people in your network remember you and like you. Many people find it difficult to network with a wide range of strangers, especially with strangers they neither go to school nor work with. What to say to start a conversation? How to keep a conversation going? What happens after the first conversation? Don't worry. It is natural to feel uneasy. Except for the few natural-born connectors, networking is not easy; it does take a lot of effort. This is especially true for people who are more introverted than extroverted. But the good news is that networking is like playing golf or driving a car—the more you do it, the better you get at it, and the more fun you have doing it.

HBS does not have a class on how to network. But when you are in an environment where most people try very hard to network, you can quickly observe who is good and who is not, what works and what doesn't. By observing the best networkers, I've seen five key elements in the formula for successful networking: interest in the other person, a sense of humor, the right attitude, consistent follow-up, and reciprocity. Some people use all five, some use just one or two.

It is worth mentioning that while there is no HBS class on networking (at least not when I was there), the last on the list, reciprocity, is very much highlighted in "negotiation" and in "power and influence" classes. The same concept is also very powerful for networking.

The first element is interest in others. Remember: me, me, me, is dull, dull, dull. As Dale Carnegie, author of the classic *How to Win Friends and Influence People*, said, "You can make more friends in two months by becoming really interested in other people than you can in two years trying to get other people interested in you . . . to be interesting, be interested."[10] This is just another way of saying Harvey Mackay's famous line, "The way to make a friend is to be one."[11]

One key way to show an interest is to talk about what the other person is excited and happy to talk about. Everyone has a favorite topic. These days in the Harvard community, it is usually family, kids, golf, sports, wine, ballroom dancing, gym, travel, or mutual friends. Once you've identified such a topic, take an interest and ask questions about it. Try to choose a topic you are truly interested in so you do not have to fake your interest. Ask why. Ask about your acquaintance's experience. Try to avoid closed (yes-or-no) questions. Listen and respond instead of talking too much about yourself.

The second key element to the formula of successful networking is a sense of humor. Good networkers often use a sense of humor on themselves. They tell funny or embarrassing stories about themselves. A sense of humor on oneself has three advantages: laughing relaxes other people—you will not risk offending other people because you are not making fun of them, and when you make fun of yourself, people feel that you are open to them. But humor, like everything else, does not work when it is forced and unnatural. So it is not necessary to be humorous if it makes you uncomfortable. Do not try to interrupt a conversation to tell an unrelated story about yourself. Also, try not to preface your story by saying, "Let me tell you something very funny." This will set up an expectation and would be embarrassing if your listeners do not find it funny.

The third element is the right attitude, to persevere even if it is not comfortable for you in the beginning. You have to convince yourself you really want to do it. Every time you give up an opportunity to meet someone, you miss an opportunity to build your network. It may also motivate you to remember that the more you do it, the easier it will become.

Once you have a nice first conversation with someone, try to follow-up so the person does not just forget the encounter. Short notes yield long results. Many successful people, including Lou Holtz (the Notre Dame football coach), Harvey Mackay, and Wheelock Whitney (who built one of the most successful U.S. brokerage firms) are all masters of short notes. "I want you to know how much I enjoyed our meeting (or your gift, your hospitality, or whatever)"; "Congratulations on your promotion (or acquisition, new job, new baby)." The notes are all handwritten, not written by a secretary. They are mailed no later than the day after the meeting or as soon as the special news arrives. It takes only a minute but it shows you really care about the relationship. It also reinforces the relationship. You will find most HBS people do the same thing, though many of them now do it through e-mail. Lastly, these notes should not be just after the first encounter or for major events. It should be done once in a while so that the relationship does not just die off.

One step beyond follow-up notes is to extend favors so you can collect later. This is often referred to as the "Law of Reciprocity," which demands that every favor must someday be repaid. Of course, this law cannot be scientifically proven or strictly enforced. There is often no material penalty for not repaying a favor. But it is very much a sacred unwritten law that most people feel it is dishonorable to break.

Favors are most effective when the following conditions apply:

- The recipient really needs or wants the favor.
- The recipient cannot easily get whatever it is from other sources.
- You can help without having to call on a major favor from someone else.
- You do not need any repayment in the near future. (It makes a favor less effective if the recipient knows that you have ulterior motives.)
- The favor does not involve money. If it does involve money, it is best if it is a sum that is insignificant to you. (Loan collection can turn a favor into animosity, especially when the sum is significant to you.)
- The one offering the favor does not feel exploited.

Favors should only be given at the right time and to the right people. Professor Kathleen K. Reardon, a leading authority on persuasion and negotiation and a subject advisor for the Harvard Business Essentials publication *Power, Influence, and Persuasion*, warns, "If you do too many things for people too often, favors cease to have significance, or may even become off-putting,"[12] and "Take care that your generosity is not being exploited by people who have no intention of repaying it."[13]

A favor can be something as simple as giving a ride that a person cannot easily obtain at that time and place. It can be advising a younger person on college applications or getting interviews at your firm. It can be helping to obtain difficult-to-get concert or sports tickets. It can be introducing somebody to the right contact for professional, personal, medical, or other matters. It can also be a very big effort like championing somebody's election campaign or saving someone from getting fired.

Besides practicing the five key elements, you can also improve your networking techniques by observing and emulating good networkers around you. Plato said each thing or idea has a perfect form. While we can never achieve the ideal form, we can attempt to come as close as we can by observing and emulating the characteristics of the ideal form. This ancient Greek advice bears some resemblance to what is preached by Anthony Robbins. Robbins is considered by many to be the U.S. leader in the science of peak performance.

Robbins has helped heads of state, Olympic and professional athletes, movie stars, and children to achieve their full potential. Some HBS graduates are Robbins followers. One of the key techniques Robbins teaches is improvement through observing and emulating the characteristics of successful people.

In the simplest form, this is what you do: Ask yourself, "Who is the most ideal networker I know? What would that person do in this situation?" Look among your friends and acquaintances, you are bound to find at least one good networker. Then you try to observe what this networker says and does. You then pretend you are that person and emulate. If you are able to do that, you can reinvent yourself and possibly become a connector!

Notes

1. Harvey Mackay, *Dig Your Well Before You Are Thirsty* (New York: Doubleday, 1999), 11.
2. Thomas J. Stanley, *The Millionaire Mind* (Kansas City: Andrews McMeel, 2001), 38.
3. For an updated report on this work, see Mark Granovetter, *Getting a Job: A Study of Contacts and Careers* (Chicago: University of Chicago Press, 1995).
4. Robert Kelley and Judith Caplan, "How Bell Labs Creates Star Performers," *Harvard Business Review* (July 1993).
5. Harvey Mackay, *Dig Your Well Before You Are Thirsty* (New York: Doubleday, 1999), 11.
6. This study was done by Andrea Frazzini, assistant professor at the University of Chicago, Lauren Cohen from Yale and Christopher Malloy from the London Business School.
7. These were their positions when I met them. Some have changed jobs since then.
8. Malcolm Gladwell, *The Tipping Point* (New York: Little, Brown, 2002).
9. Harvey Mackay, *Dig Your Well Before You Are Thirsty* (New York: Doubleday, 1999), 19.
10. Dale Carnegie, *How to Win Friends and Influence People* (New York: Pocket Books, 1998). (Originally published 1936.)
11. Harvey Mackay, *Dig Your Well Before You Are Thirsty* (New York: Doubleday, 1999), 11
12. Jennifer McFarland, "Four Bulletproof Strategies for Handling Office Politics," *Harvard Management Update* (May 2001), 2.
13. Harvard Business Essentials, *Power, Influence, and Persuasion* (Boston: Harvard Business School Press, 2005), 26.

5

IT IS BIGGER THAN YOU

PRIORITIZE

While almost all HBS alumni think very highly of themselves, they are also the first to admit that life is full of constraints and conflicts. It can be a meeting that goes on and on while the family is waiting for a major celebration. It can be a critical strategy decision that has to be made quickly without enough data. It can be such a flood of data that it's hard to see where to start. It can be a conflict between the current rush assignment and the new grand idea that just occurred to the boss (or, worse, the boss's boss) today.

Resource constraints and conflicts are inevitable. These constraints are well-illustrated by the case study method. The tremendous amount of case workload, the time conflicts between work and private life, the lack of perfect data despite the significant amount of background given in each case study, all reinforce the reality that people are always constrained in some way. The keys to managing resource constraints and conflicts include discipline, courage, and tools.

Discipline

Discipline means that instead of immediately committing to and attempting to do everything, one remembers to take a step back to question if the resources can adequately meet the demand. If not, one must have the *courage* to discuss the constraint with the others involved and use the appropriate *tools* to prioritize and manage the compromise.

Courage

Courage means to be able to highlight the possible constraint and work out a solution with the other people involved. These other people could be your spouse, children, boss, clients, or colleagues. This is especially important in managing upward. Often, especially early on in their careers, people are so anxious to prove themselves that they do not have the courage to bring up the issue of resource constraints. It is always better to have the courage to discuss the constraint up front and early rather than to fail to deliver what is promised.

Tools

Some of the key tools for prioritizing and managing constraints:

- Seeing the big picture
- Setting expectations
- Minding the 80/20 Rule

Seeing the Big Picture

There are two categories of big pictures:

○ *Personal versus business.* Despite the competitiveness of people at HBS, most value family life very highly. They generally believe the old saying, "At the point of death, no one regrets not spending enough time at work but many regret not spending enough time with family." Hence, the big picture is when there is a conflict between personal and business lives, though career pressure pushes business to the forefront, it is best to keep track of the big picture and decide accordingly.

○ *Within business.* Whenever there is a conflict for resources—such as what data to analyze first, what project to do first, what topic to discuss first, and how to avoid digression during a meeting—it is useful to ask, "What is the big picture?" and "What is the central issue?" This often helps prioritize data, projects, and discussions.

Setting Expectations

This is a true story: When I was a new consultant, my boss asked me to get some data for him in a week's time. Eager to please, I told him I could give it to him in half that time. Unfortunately, it took longer than I thought. After three days, I told him it would take me another two days. But I was confident I could finish before the original deadline he'd given me. I was expecting that he would be OK with that since I would still be ahead of what he originally asked for. But he was furious. Because I had told him to expect the data in three days, he had planned on getting the data early. His plans would need to be totally revamped because of my delays. He was upset and so was I.

From then on, I never forgot the importance of setting the appropriate expectations. Two rules I now abide by at all times:

- *Better be safe than sorry.* It is better not to be overaggressive in setting expectations. Be a pleasant surprise rather than an unpleasant disappointment.
- *Work often takes longer than seems likely up front.* In my case, I find the 1.5-times factor very accurate. That is, if I think a piece of work should take Y number of days, the actual time needed is usually Y multiplied by 1.5. This factor is not scientifically proven and may be specific to my own style. You may want to find your own factor.

Minding the 80/20 Rule

There is a rule of thumb that has worked time and again for me. This is the 80/20 rule, which says 80 percent of the total output is or can be generated by roughly 20 percent of the total input. For example, the following observations are probably true:

- 80 percent of your company's sales come from the top 20 percent of your customers.
- 80 percent of your company's revenues come from 20 percent of your sales force.
- 80 percent of your payroll goes to 20 percent of your staff.

The 80/20 rule was first developed by Vilfredo Pareto (1848–1923), a French-Italian sociologist, economist, and philosopher. While researching economic conditions in his native Italy, Pareto determined that 20 percent of the population owned 80 percent of the land. Subsequently, while working in his garden, he discovered that about 80 percent of his peas came from just 20 percent of his plants. Based on these and other observations, he determined that for any series of elements under study, a small fraction of the number of elements usually accounts for a large fraction of the effect. Over time, Pareto's observation became generalized as the 80/20 rule.[1]

Naturally, 80 and 20 are not rigid numbers. These are estimates that mean that the bulk (usually over 60 percent) of results can be attributed to a small fraction (usually less than 40 percent) of the input.

The 80/20 rule is extremely helpful for prioritization. It means that the top 20 percent should be given the most attention–it can be the top 20 percent of the customers, 20 percent of the data for analysis, 20 percent of the staff who are getting the highest pay.

An example from my early consulting experience solidified my belief in this rule: I was working for a relatively unsophisticated client in China. I found that its sales department evenly distributed sales staff time among the customers, so each customer got the same amount of time and service from the sales staff. As a result, each salesperson was assigned 10 customers and instructed to serve all of them equally well. While the company overall was profitable, revenues and profitability were not growing. When we interviewed the major customers, we found that they felt my client's sales staff was "all right" but not "stellar" in their service. They did not feel my client valued them. Therefore, even though they continued to buy from the client, they were also giving business to other companies that were giving them "similar or better service." When we interviewed the small customers, they were very impressed by my client valuing them as if they were a big customer. However, although they wanted to buy more, their size did not allow them to increase their orders by much.

In addition to ineffective customer service, such allocation of resources is also inefficient from a customer profitability perspective, as shown in Figure 5.1.

In the end, the study recommended a reallocation of resources—80 percent of the sales force time should be spent on the 20 percent of major or growing customers.

Another example of the 80/20 rule came up in my recent study on a property investment company, as shown in Figure 5.2.

Figure 5.1 Return on Sales Effort

Average annual salary of a salesperson: US$24,000

Number of customers served by each salesperson: 10

Average salesperson cost per customer: US$24,000/10 = US$2,400

Gross margins (costs of goods): 80% revenues

Customer ranking	Annual sales generated by the client (A)	Revenues growth from previous year	Costs of goods 80% × (A)	Salesperson costs to serve customer	% Customer profit (Revenues − costs of goods − salesperson costs)/Revenues
No. 1 (Biggest customer)	US$5,000,000	0%	$4,000,000	$2,400	Almost 20%
No. 20	US$3,200,000	5%	$2,560,000	$2,400	Almost 20%
No. 308 (Smallest customer)	US$15,000	1%	$12,000	$2,400	4% (profit is probably negative if other costs like transportation, order processing, and so on are included)

Low-Hanging Fruit

Sometimes quick results are better than big results. This can be due to a variety of reasons: the need to build credibility for yourself, your team, or your project; a business crisis such as the need for immediate cash; morale; or too much time and effort needed to get big results. In such cases, instead of

Figure 5.2 Rental Returns

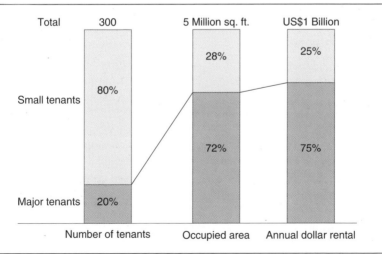

applying the 80/20 rule, which focuses on the biggest impact, it may be more effective to focus on capturing the "low-hanging fruit." As the term implies, it means exploiting the opportunities that are easiest to capture. For example, I was once involved as the consultant for reengineering a state-owned petrochemical company in one of the Asian countries. The company was experiencing explosive growth and found that it could not hire enough qualified people to support that growth. The goal of the project was to redesign key processes and functions to make better use of the available human resources. The company had about 20 offices and refineries across the country. When planning the project, we had a few options. Here is a simplified summary of the options we considered:

Options	Key Considerations
1. Start with the largest offices and refineries	80/20 rule
2. Start all at the same time	To shorten the total duration of project
3. Start with a small refinery that has outdated processes and a significant manpower shortage and then roll out to rest of company	Find "low-hanging fruit" that can help build credibility for project

In the end, we chose approach 3. This is because some senior client executives were skeptical of the project and the involvement of expensive external consultants. By quickly achieving results in a small refinery, we built credibility that made it feasible to get support for a rollout to the rest of the company. We were also able to gather some best practices that were useful as we rolled the project out.

Plan B

It is obvious that many factors are beyond our control, both in our personal lives and in business. Plan B means to have a backup plan, to have a plan for the worst-case scenario, to have a plan to turn to when your assumptions turn out to be wrong. It can be completely different from the original plan or it can be a moderation, change, or adaptation of the original plan should that plan become infeasible. While this seems logical and natural, the reality is that Plan B is often either forgotten or not done properly. This can be because of negligence, wishful thinking that Plan A will work just as planned, or lack of resources.

It is true that Plan B, when developed, is very often not used. But Plan B is like car insurance. Many people have the insurance but never claim enough to cover the premium paid. This is how insurance companies can make money. However, you do want the insurance just in case you get into an accident. The chance of a major accident may be slim. But you want insurance just in case it happens. This is the rationale behind insisting on having a Plan B.

I keep a story and an adage in mind to remind me of Plan B. The story (which is true): There's a U.S. television reality show called *The Apprentice*, hosted by the high-profile real estate tycoon Donald Trump. Each season, a group of contestants including business school graduates, entrepreneurs, lawyers, and so on have to solve many business challenges under a tight time frame. Contestants are eliminated until the final two. Then there is a final challenge and a winner is selected from the two. The winner will get an apprenticeship from Trump.

In the season finale, the two finalists were asked to each plan a big charity fundraising activity. One finalist was an HBS graduate with a doctorate from another leading school, who had been outstanding throughout the competition. He was definitely the front-runner going into the finals. He was asked to plan an outdoor charity event within a very limited time. While he was planning, somebody informed him that the weather forecast indicated possible rain on the day of the event. However, working under tremendous time pressure, he ignored the information. The day came and rain was pouring down. He had no Plan B. He had to scramble to change everything in his Plan A. Needless to say, he paid a high price for the mistake.

In addition to this story, I find Murphy's Law (an oft-quoted Western adage) useful as a reminder of the need of a Plan B. Murphy's Law has many versions, but the one I go by whenever I plan is "What can go wrong will go wrong," especially when you least expect and can least afford it. Of course, I don't mean you have to have a Plan B for everything that "can go wrong." That would be too arduous and too costly. The factors to consider in determining whether a Plan B should be done and how much effort should be put into it can be expressed in a qualitative formula:

$$\text{Plan B?} = \text{Possible impact of no Plan B} \\ \times \text{Probability of a need to execute Plan B} \\ \div \text{Effort required to develop Plan B}$$

With a "qualitative formula," hard data and numbers are not necessary. It is just an aid to a qualitative decision. The formula is self-explanatory:

- The larger the possible impact if certain assumptions or parameters do go wrong, the bigger the need for a detailed Plan B. Using the story of the would-be apprentice, it should have been obvious that if it rained, it would be impossible to use the outdoor venue and setup and to do any of the outdoor events planned. So the impact would have been major and a Plan B for bad weather should have been developed to a significant level of detail.
- The higher the probability for certain assumptions and parameters to go wrong, the bigger the need for a detailed Plan B. Again, using the same story, given the weather forecast, the probability of rain was high and a Plan B was called for.
- The smaller the effort for Plan B, the bigger is the argument to have a more detailed plan B. If a detailed Plan B requires millions of dollars and significant time and energy to plan, it may be natural to take the risk with only a very broad Plan B. One option is not to have a specific Plan B, but to assign resources that can be deployed when necessary. A client of mine always appoints a "Navy Seals" team for its major projects. The team is ready to be deployed to solve any unplanned problems for major projects.

The final decision on the need for Plan B is a judgment based on putting all three factors together.

Ass-U-Me—Trite but True

I learned one thing early on in my career: if in doubt, ask. For many different reasons, including overconfidence, lack of confidence to ask, or simply lack of time, many people have a tendency to make unfounded assumptions. Whenever I make assumptions, I always remind myself of some words of wisdom I learned from my superiors very early on in my consulting career: "Do you know what happens when you assume? You make an Ass-(out of)-u-(and)-me." Needless to say, these words of wisdom came after I made some poor assumptions in some consulting projects. You can imagine the damage to your credibility if you are questioned on your assumptions and you cannot defend them, as in this exchange:

> CLIENT (OR YOUR SUPERIOR): I see in your strategy study you assume inflation of 5 percent a year in the next few years. What makes you say that?

You: That's the historical inflation rate.

Client: Why did you assume it will be the same in the next few years?

You: (silence because any answer will look bad: *I had no time, I was sloppy and did not think hard . . .*)

Therefore, it is important to remember that any assumption can be questioned. So, whenever you make an assumption, you must ask yourself— can I defend this assumption? Possible defense includes a credible source (such as government or expert published research data, or interviews with experts or the client's senior management) or a clear logic (such as the historical rate is studied over 50 years and is a good medium-term average, or sensitivity analysis indicates that inflation has very little impact on our decisions and hence we did not spend too much time on it). If you have a source or logic, others may still disagree. But their disagreement will lead into a discussion designed to refine the assumption, and you will not lose credibility as a result of making it.

Note

1. Ethan M. Raisial and Paul N. Friga, *The McKinsey Mind* (New York: McGraw-Hill, 2002).

PART II

OPERATIONS

6

PROCESS

THERE IS A PROCESS FOR EVERYTHING

Part II of this book is about HBS's skills and tools for managing operations. Instead of immediately going through each function, this section starts with the discussion of an overarching operations management tool called *process management*, which is powerful for thinking-through and optimizing any function. After process management, I discuss some key principles in managing human resources, marketing, sales, and finance that are critical but not covered by process management.

Formally, HBS defines a *process* as "any part of the organization that takes inputs and transforms them into outputs of greater value to the organization than the original inputs."[1] Informally, I find it useful to think of process a series of steps, supported by the appropriate tools and systems, by which work gets done.

At the functional level, a significant amount of work gets done through processes. Here are some examples of typical processes in various functions:

- In human resources: recruitment and hiring, annual evaluation, sick leave application
- In finance: expense reimbursement, budgeting
- In manufacturing: production, materials planning

- In sales and marketing: annual marketing planning, pre-sales, sales, post-sales
- In back office operations (as in a bank): loan approval, bad loan collection

In all these examples, a series of steps, employing various supporting tools and systems, need to be taken to complete the work. By being able to see and understand work done as a process and to analyze key processes, ineffective and inefficient steps, policies, tools, systems, and paperwork can be identified and improved where possible. This skill is sometimes referred to as "process reengineering."

The key tools for understanding and analyzing a process include a set of best practice principles that help question and identify inefficiencies and ineffectiveness, and a process mapping technique that makes it possible to analyze processes using those principles.

BEST PRACTICE PRINCIPLES

This section lists the best practice principles that I have found most useful when analyzing process efficiency and effectiveness. An *efficient* process is one that is low cost and fast. An *effective* process is one that delivers the intended outcomes. The first three practices listed here are more related to efficiency and the last two are more related to effectiveness. I start with the efficiency-related principles even though the effectiveness-related ones are more fundamental to a process because my experience has shown that the former are easier to apply and more frequently applied. I have phrased the principles in the form of questions so it is clearer how they can be applied when analyzing a process.

- Are the steps in the process done right the first time?
- Is waiting time minimized?
- Is the weakest link as strong as it can be?
- Is the process doing what it is supposed to do?
- Is authorization appropriate?

Are the steps in the process done right the first time?

Work should be done correctly the first time, and mechanisms should be built in to help ensure correct action. This will reduce the need for quality inspection, rework, waiting time for rework, wastage, and so on, all of which are low-value-added and increase the time and cost needed to get the process completed. Checking and even correction mechanisms designed and built into the process can be very powerful in ensuring "right first time." The spelling checker and automated spelling correction in Microsoft Word is an example. Other typical examples for white-collar work are templates and checklists. Examples for manufacturing include color coding and workstations designed to prevent workers from making mistakes.

Is waiting time minimized?

Waiting time means time has passed with no value being added to the products or services that need to be produced. For a manufacturing process, waiting time will mean larger work-in-progress inventory. Inventory means the cash invested in making the inventory is not yet ready to be converted into income. Inventory also incurs interest costs because of the money invested in it. Outside manufacturing waiting time means increasing the amount of time needed to complete a process. This means low efficiency and poor customer service if the waiting time affects the customer.

Is the weakest link as strong as it can be?

When I took the HBS class on operations, we were required to read a best-selling business novel called *The Goal*. The book was almost 400 pages long and the first 200 pages were more or less trying to illustrate a single basic point:

capacity of a process = capacity of its biggest bottleneck

A bottleneck is a factor that limits production.[1] In other words the weakest link (bottleneck) of a process will limit and hence determine how much a process can produce. A simple example: say the process of publishing this business book has only two steps: writing the book by me and printing the book by my publisher. I can write a book every two years. My publisher can get any finished book printed within one month. However, even though my publisher can print in such a short time, the process is limited by my speed. I am the bottleneck. If I'm the only author on tap, the publisher can put out only one book every two years because of my speed, as illustrated in Table 6.1.

Table 6.1 Time to Market

Step 1: writing a book (2 years)	Step 2: printing (1 month)	Published date
1 January 2008 to 31 December 2009	1 January 2010 to 31 January 2010	31 January 2010
1 January 2010 to 31 December 2011	1 January 2012 to 31 January 2012	31 January 2012
1 January 2012 to 31 December 2013	1 January 2014 to 31 January 2014	31 January 2014

Two technical terms are useful when trying to understand the relationship between a bottleneck and the whole process:

- *Cycle time.* Cycle time is the time between two output units generated by a step of the process or the entire process. The cycle time of a process is the same as the cycle time of the bottleneck. The step of writing (the bottleneck step) and the entire process (writing and printing) will both have a cycle time of two years per book. Notice how the cycle time for printing is not a factor in this consideration.
- *Capacity.* Capacity of a process is the maximum rate of output of the entire process. Capacity is measured in units of output per unit of time. The inverse of cycle time is capacity. This means the capacity of writing and the capacity of the entire process look like this:

> Inverse of two years per book
> = one book per two years
> = half a book per year

If process capacity is the inverse of process cycle time and process cycle time is determined by bottleneck cycle time, then process capacity is determined by bottleneck cycle time.

Once this relationship is clear, then the importance of identifying, understanding, and managing bottlenecks is self-evident.

Is the process doing what it is supposed to do?

When processes are first established, they are usually quite effective in serving their intended purpose. However, over time, processes can become ineffective if they are not updated to keep abreast of changes inside and outside the company. Reasons for failure to update could include inertia, inability to see the need for change, inability to make a change, or resistance to the changes in power bases that would result from changing the process.

One key example of ineffective process I have seen in a number of clients and HBS case studies is the outdated sales resource allocation process. This problem is vividly described in the *Harvard Business Review* article "The New Science of Sales Force Productivity," where the authors used a fictitious sales manager, Bob, to summarize the issue of the old process that is used by many companies in allocating their salespeople's time:[2]

> Bob Brody leaned back in his chair, frowning. Corporate wanted another 8% increase in sales. . . . Ah for the good old days, when he could just announce a 10% target, spread it like peanut butter over all his territories, and then count on the sales reps (to use their personal relationships) for each region or product line to deliver. . . . Today, the purchasing departments of Bob's customers used algorithms to choose vendors for routine buys; pure economics often trumped personal relationships. . . . Bob was overwhelmed.

Here's a real-life though somewhat disguised example of the same problem. One of my clients, a property investment firm (call it Company P) generates revenues from rental income from its shopping malls. Company P's share price was depressed due to below-market revenue growth. The consulting project found that the sales process was becoming ineffective:

- Historically, Company P's sales team has always been autonomous and powerful. It has been in charge of the entire process of rental from tenant identification to rental negotiation to rent collection ever since the company started.
- The process was effective in the past when the market was simpler—a rental deal meant agreeing on a fixed monthly amount. However, as the market became more complex, rental deals also became more complex. For example, in addition to a fixed monthly rent, sometimes there is a variable turnover rent that is paid as a percentage of the tenant's actual revenues if revenues for the month exceed a certain fixed minimum threshold. Or some key anchor tenants will demand an up-front subsidy or loan for renovation or a two- or even three-year rent-free period.

- Company P's retail sales team did not have the analytical capability to assess these terms. As a result, subsequent analyses showed that many of the terms they signed were unprofitable because the turnover rent threshold, up-front subsidy, or loan to the tenant was too high.
- Another problem with the process was the market itself, which was getting more competitive with many more shopping malls. It became critical for Company P to differentiate by signing up unique, successful overseas retail brands and concepts. But the sales team did not have the experience of actively identifying and marketing to such retailers.

The consulting project recommended some key changes, including a process for identifying and marketing to overseas target tenants and involvement of the finance department in approval and monitoring of complex rental deals.

Is authorization appropriate?

Many processes require authorization. For example, a payment process in finance may require signatures from the department manager applying for the payment, the finance manager approving the payment, and the finance director for signing the checks. Such checks and balances are necessary for risk management. However, a process that requires authorization by people who do not have the appropriate qualifications can result in ineffectiveness or sometimes inefficiency. It is important to question and challenge each authorization on the grounds of need and effectiveness. For example, I was consulting for one of the biggest state-owned banks in China. The bank had a bad debt problem and wanted to improve its loan approval process. After some analysis, we discovered that the loan approval committee consisted of a large number of people who were very senior at the bank but who were not trained in risk management. To make it worse, many of them tried to avoid these meetings or put them low on their priority list. As a result, it was very time-consuming to schedule loan approval meetings (which of course added to the lead time for loan approval) and the decisions taken at these meetings were often suboptimal. By redefining the composition of the loan approval committee, the bank was able to not only improve the quality of the decisions but also reduce the time for loan approval (thereby improving customer service) as it became easier to schedule loan approval meetings.

PROCESS MAPPING

Process mapping is an important tool for visualizing, understanding, and improving a process. It has two key components:

- Construction of process maps or flowcharts.
- Analysis of key components of the process maps.

Usually two maps are drawn for each process—one before process reengineering (or process improvement), and one after. Best practice principles are applied to each step depicted in the before map to understand how the process can be improved. People sometimes refer to the analysis of key components as "off-map analysis" or "key analysis," and I find these terms useful even though they are not official.

Types of Maps

Process maps come in three general types. The choice depends on the process involved. It is easiest to illustrate process mapping by examples.

Basic Maps

Expanding on the earlier example about my capacity for writing and publishing books, Figure 6.1 illustrates mapping that process.

Though some professional standards for flowchart shapes, such as a rectangle for a process step and an inverted triangle for inventory, have been established, I have never felt it necessary to follow any of them strictly. The key is to clearly define and be consistent in your own usage.

Process improvement can be done by applying the best practice principles to this map and starting from the most time-consuming step. These are some of the key "best practice" questions to ask:

- The biggest bottleneck is text writing. Can the text writing time be reduced? Possible solutions could be hiring one more nanny to reduce distraction from my young baby, hiring an assistant to help organize research materials, or reducing the family vacation.
- A major inefficiency is rework. Can the number of reworks be reduced? My publisher and I could brainstorm together on how to

Figure 6.1 Process Map for a Book

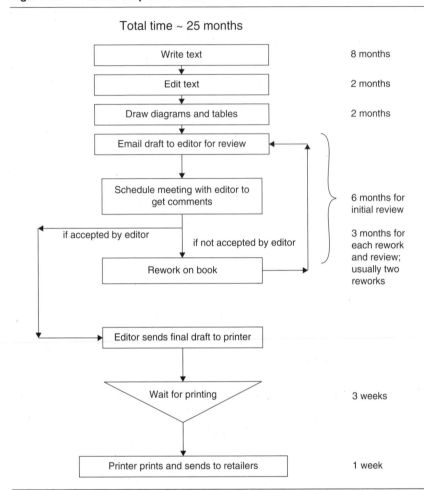

reduce rework, such as the publisher generating a checklist of requirements, or me submitting each chapter as it is finished so I can take the
feedback into consideration as I continue to write more chapters.
- Can review time by the editor be reduced?
- Can waiting time at the printer be reduced?

Multi-Party Maps

For processes where a lot of different parties (people or departments) are
involved, the format illustrated in Figure 6.2 can be used.

Figure 6.2 Multi-Party Process Map

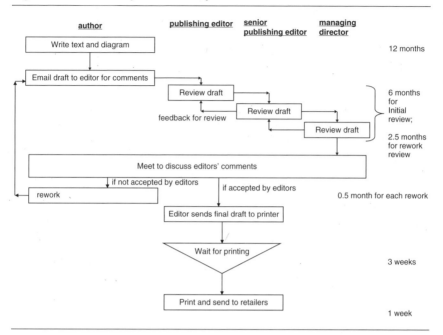

This format can highlight any inefficiency due to multiple parties' involvement, such as excessive authorization and review, handoffs back and forth leading to waiting time and rework, and so on. This example is a simple one, with few parties involved. I have seen processes where so many parties are involved with so many handoffs that arrows were running all over the page. This usually indicates significant opportunities for improvement.

Black and White Space Maps

A black and white space map is most useful to highlight low- and non-value-added waiting time, rework time, and other delays in the process. It is also useful for identifying bottlenecks and inefficiencies. Focusing on rework review in the book publishing process produces the map shown in Figure 6.3.

A few points to note on this map:

- The horizontal axis is time elapsed that affects the critical path.[3] It should be drawn to scale as much as possible so it is easy to see the process visually. It has a lot of impact when the color for non-value-added steps dominates the map.

Figure 6.3 Black and White Space Map

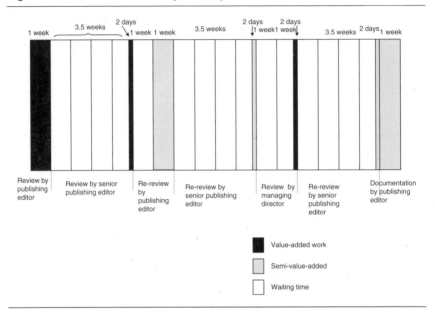

- The value-added steps are shaded in one color (black is my prefer-ence.) Some steps are obviously value-added, such as physically writing the book, approvals necessary for risk management, reports required by law, quality checks for mistakes that could not be systematically and perfectly avoided, and so on.
- The non-value-added steps are shaded in a contrasting color (white is my preference.) Some steps are obviously non-value-added such as waiting time, rubber-stamp type approvals, rework for mistakes that could have been systematically avoided in the first place, and so on.
- You may find it necessary to have a third category—semi-value-added. For example, if the re-review by the publishing editor after review by the senior editor is 95 percent reading the comments and only 5 percent adding further insights, then it can be seen as "semi-value-added." Usually, I like to use gray for the steps that cannot be easily eliminated (as they are not totally non-value-added) but maybe can be reduced or streamlined to increase process efficiency.

As discussed, best practice principles are applied to the process maps to help identify areas for improvement. It is worth noting that best practice principles are applied not only after the "before" map is fully drawn, but also during the research and the drawing of the maps. For example, if there seem to be a lot of complaints about a certain step in the process, then special attention should be paid to verify (with other interviews or analysis steps) and highlight this issue in the "before" map.

Besides best practice principles, benchmarking similar processes within the company or at other companies is also a powerful tool. Benchmarking can help identify issues, stimulate creative solutions, and convince the organization of the need for change. This is especially useful if an organization is facing a new challenge and does not know how to adapt or create a new process to respond. A major liquor client of mine spent millions of dollars a few years ago to benchmark strategy-planning processes of leading companies around the world. The key reason was the CEO's decision that the company's top-down strategic planning process, whereby each business unit was given a target to be met, was no longer sufficient as the differences and the level of competition of the different markets increased. He needed to understand how leading companies did their strategy planning in order to design a new process and to convince his organization of the validity and need for the change.

An analogy for process reengineering is plastic surgery. There are usually two maps: before and after the surgery. To decide what to do in the surgery, classic universal beauty standards are available to assess the "before face": wrinkle-free skin, straight nose, and the like. But sometimes, perhaps because the patient cannot describe what the new face should look like, then benchmarks like "the lips of movie star Angelina Jolie" will be used. Finally, some analysis may need to be done in addition to the exterior of the face, for example, bone or muscle structure of the face, or levels of blood pressure, as part of the surgery. Such analysis will be analogous to the "off-map analysis" to be discussed in the next section.

"Off-Map" Analysis

Process mapping is an important tool for visualizing and defining the steps in the process. However, often, more in-depth analysis needs to be done on certain steps of the process. The analysis focuses on understanding and resolving any issue found in the process map. The analysis often results in recommendations for tools, systems, or automation.

Simple Analysis

Figure 6.4 shows an example of simple analysis: understanding the relative severity of different causes of inefficiency. Using the book example in the basic map section, the bottleneck is the step "writing the text." To determine how

Figure 6.4 Bar Chart for Simple Analysis

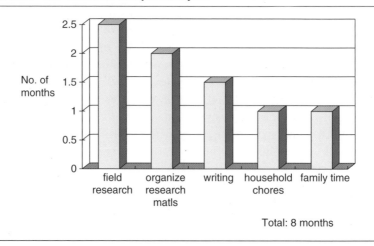

Total: 8 months

to reduce the time needed, off-map analysis can be done to dive into this step of the process.

More in-depth analysis can be done on each of the items, such as what is taking up so much research time. Solutions such as outsourcing or automation can then be identified to reduce the time.

More Advanced Analysis

Sometimes, when you have enough data, more advanced analysis can be done. A very good example was given in the *Harvard Business Review* article "The New Science of Sales Force Productivity."[4] Michael Pilot, then president of a unit of General Electric, was trying to solve the sort of client prioritization process problem highlighted by the fictitious Bob mentioned earlier on:

Problem Pilot faced: "The company's field sales managers even manually classified all the names in the division's database as either high priority or low priority . . . (relying) on telephone books . . . newspapers . . . signs on trucks as they went by or signs on buildings . . . (Pilot) knew that GE Commercial Finance had to 'put some science into it.'"

To improve the account prioritization process: "Pilot asked his field managers to create a list of . . . criteria that they believed would correlate with the customer's likelihood of doing business with GE. He took the 14 features they came up with, ran regression equations against the database of transactions and identified six criteria that had high correlations. If a prospective customer tested well on those six criteria . . . the probability that it would do business with GE is high."

Improvement: Pilot said, "We found that the top 30% of prospective customers were three times more likely to do a deal with us than the bottom 70% . . . yet only about half of them were previously classified as high priority by sales managers."

Data Sources

The data sources for process maps and analysis are very similar to the data sources for strategy study discussed in Part III of this book. Here, it is enough to highlight some of the key points:

- *Interviews are a key source of data.* Very few companies document their processes in detail. Even when they do, what is on paper may sometimes be very different from actual practice. Hence, interviews with people involved in the process are a key source of data, especially for the maps.
- *Quantification is important.* Quantification measures the extent of any inefficiency or ineffectiveness, helping you see how big any problem is and hence the priorities, and convince others of the need for change. For example, if rework is high, you would want to know how many times things go back for rework, how much time each rework takes, how much material is wasted, how much money can be saved if the process is changed, and the like.
- *Sampling is a useful tool.* Interviewees sometimes give you conflicting descriptions of the process, or find it impossible to give you the information you need. This can be because they are trying to hide issues or because the process is truly messy. In such cases, one tool I have found useful is to do sampling, as described in more detail in Chapter 12.
- *Identifying root causes of any issue is important.* This is self-explanatory. The key skill is "asking why five times," and is discussed in Appendix B.

Notes

1. Ann E. Grey and Leonard James, "Process Fundamentals," *Harvard Business Review* (September 2007).

2. Dianne Ledingham, Mark Kovac, and Heidi Locke Simon, "The New Science of Sales Force Productivity," *Harvard Business Review* (September 2006); quote on p. 1 of article.

3. *Critical path* is the process or the sequence of steps that determine the process time. For example, in the book writing example, there may be other activities like payments and meetings. But these activities are not on the "critical path" as they do not affect the process time.

4. Dianne Ledingham, Mark Kovac, and Heidi Locke Simon, "The New Science of Sales Force Productivity," *Harvard Business Review* (September 2006); quotes in this section are from p. 2 of the article.

7

HUMAN RESOURCES

AIM TO BE THE STUPIDEST BOSS

If you ask the HBS graduates who are business owners or hired chief executives (and in fact any seasoned business owners) what the single most difficult thing in managing a business is, the answer would most likely be "people." Hiring, training, motivating, and retaining people are extremely important but challenging. To me, the best business is one that generates income without any employees. That's why I like writing books and investing in real estate and stock markets. These lines let me work largely on my own.

Why is the "people" issue so difficult? First, you have to find the right people. That is critical to success. For the book *Good to Great*, Jim Collins, a best-selling author and formerly a faculty member at Stanford Business School, and his team of 20 researchers spent five years on in-depth analysis of almost 30 major companies, trying to understand what the best CEOs did to make their good companies into truly great companies. This is one of his major findings:

First Who . . . Then What. We expected that good-to-great leaders would begin by setting a new vision and strategy. We found instead that they first got the right people on the bus, the wrong people off the bus, and the right people in the right seats—and *then* they figured out where to drive it. The old adage "People are your most important asset" turns out to be wrong. People are not your most important asset. The right people are.[1]

Later, Collins adds, "When (we asked one of the good-to-great CEOs) to name the top five factors that led to the transition from mediocrity to excellence, (he) said, 'One would be people. Two would be people. Three would be people. Four would be people.' "[2]

David Ogilvy, the legendary advertising giant and founder of the major global advertising agency Ogilvy and Mather, believed that hiring the right people could even mean hiring people more capable than the hirer. It was said that whenever someone was appointed to head an office at his firm, Ogilvy would give him a Russian nesting doll. These dolls open to reveal a smaller doll, which opens to reveal a yet smaller doll and so on. Inside the smallest doll was a note from Ogilvy: "If each of us hires people who are smaller than we are, we shall become a company of *dwarfs*. But if each of us hires people who are bigger than we are, we shall become a company of *giants*."[3]

Jack Welch, ex-CEO of General Electric, an HBS graduate and a man many revere as one of the most respected and successful CEOs in U.S. history, shares the same philosophy. When asked what counsel he would give junior executives to help them become future leaders, Welch answered: "The biggest advice I give people is you cannot do these jobs alone. You've got to be very comfortable with the brightest human beings alive on your team. And if you do that, you get the world by the tail. . . . Always get the best people. If you haven't one who's good, you are short-changing yourself."[4]

Of course, this may or may not be applicable if you are a middle or even a senior hired manager. Since you are not the ultimate boss, the company culture and your own boss's attitude affect how you might want to hire. HBS teaches its students to be realistic. It would be unrealistic if you were a middle manager to go to your boss and say, "I really don't know the strategy for my department. But just let me hire the best team and then we can figure out what to do with my department." You will probably get fired. It would also be unrealistic to advise you to hire people smarter than you are if your company does not reward this behavior and your boss does not have the same vision as Collins, Ogilvy, and Welch. A friend of mine got fired when his boss decided the friend's assistant could do his job at a much lower salary.

HIRE SLOWLY, FIRE DECISIVELY

As Harvey Mackay says, "It isn't the people you fire that make your life miserable, it's the people you don't." You should take your time to find the right people. You should give each employee a detailed description of your expectations and follow-up with regular feedback. When things do not work out, you must be decisive and let the person go. To build the best business, you need the best people, as Jim Collins found out from his in-depth analysis:[5]

"When in doubt don't hire—keep looking." As the CEO of the companies that went from good to great told Collins, "You don't compromise. We find another way to get through until we find the right people."

"When you know you need to make people change, act." But how do you know "when you know"? According to Collins's research, two key questions can help: Would you hire the person again? And if the person came to you to resign, would you feel disappointed or relieved?

Jeffrey Fox, an HBS alumnus and a best-selling author, shows why making the right hiring decision is so important by explaining the cost of mishiring:

Mishiring costs include compensation paid, termination settlements, recruitment expenses, management time, and placement fees. The biggest costs of a mishire are harder to identify and quantify, but they are real: costs to replace, disruption to the organization, management errors, lost opportunities, strategy failure, wasted training, and damaged morale.[6]

Jim Collins explains why firing decisively is important:

"All the time and energy we spend on that (wrong hire to try to improve performance) siphons energy away from developing and working with all the right people. . . . Letting the wrong people hang around is unfair to all the right people, as they inevitably find themselves compensating for the inadequacies of the wrong people. Worse, it can drive away the best people. Strong performers are intrinsically motivated by performance, and when they see their efforts impeded by carrying extra weight, they eventually become frustrated. . . . (It's) equally unfair to the people who need to (be let go.) For every minute you allow a person to continue holding a seat when you know that person will not make it in the end, you're stealing a portion of his life, time that he could spend finding a better place where he could flourish.[7]

Jack Welch is also a best practice guru of this philosophy. When he was at General Electric, Welch personally interviewed anyone who was hired from the outside for any of the top 500 posts, not just the few posts of his direct reports. This is because he understands the cost of a wrong hire. If the mistake of mishiring was made, he also made sure the system was set up to make appropriate correction swiftly and decisively. At Welch's General Electric, all employees were more or less classified into A, B, and C class depending on their capability. At a meeting attended by General Electric's 500 top operating managers, Welch said:

> Too many of you work hard to make C's (into) B's. It is a wheel-spinning exercise. Push C's on to B companies or C companies, and they'll do just fine. . . . We're an A company. We want only A players. We can get anyone we want. Take care of your best. Reward them. Promote them. Pay them well. Give them a lot of (stock) options and don't spend all that time trying to get C's to be B's. Move C's out early. It's a contribution.[8]

Just as Collins suggests, Welch considered firing the C's quickly a contribution not just to General Electric but to the C employees. Employees whose capabilities were C grade for General Electric might do well in other organizations where different capabilities were required. I have seen many people who did not do well in consulting end up very successful in sales or in stock trading where different skills are critical.

But firing decisively is not easy. Even to this day, after all my business school education, sometimes I am less decisive than I should be. Case in point—I have someone on staff in my company now. He is extremely loyal and hardworking. But he is just not efficient and he keeps making mistakes. I find myself spending a lot of time catching and correcting his mistakes. I have been thinking about firing him for the last two months. I know I am committing the classic mistake described by Jim Collins in his book:

> We've all experienced or observed the following scenario. We have a wrong person . . . and we know it. Yet we wait, we delay, we try alternatives, we give a third and fourth chance, we hope that the situation would improve, we invest time in trying to properly manage

the person, we build little systems to compensate for his shortcomings, and so forth. But the situation doesn't improve. When we go home, we find our energy diverted by thinking (or talking to our spouses) about that person. . . . Indeed, if we're honest with ourselves, the reason we wait too long often has less to do with concern for that person and more to do with our own convenience. He's doing an okay job and it would be a huge hassle to replace him, so we avoid the issue.[9]

If you have not been a manager, you may not have experienced this. But keep it in mind. When you are a manager, you may see yourself falling into this trap. It is hard to avoid, but at least you should be aware of it—that will at least help you act sooner than you otherwise might.

DON'T PLAY THE SLOT MACHINE

Hiring the right people and firing the wrong people is only half the battle. Once you have employees, you need to put significant and continuous effort into retaining and developing them. An HBS classmate once commented in class: "My ex-boss taught me that to focus only on recruiting and not retention and development will be like playing the slot machine—you put a lot of resources into recruiting and you leave it to luck to get a few, if any, wins."

Losing a good staff member is costly. Direct costs include loss of productivity during the transition period, mourning and insecure coworkers, and a costly candidate search and then training of the new recruit. Indirectly, high staff turnover will affect the company's ability to attract top recruits. High turnover is often seen by recruits as a sign of organizational problems.

The better the employees, the more costly they are to lose, and the more difficult it is to retain them. While money is always a consideration, competent and capable people look for much more. At HBS, whole courses address the topic of management and leadership as related to staff morale and retention. Here are the points that I have found most useful:

- Tell them
- Groom them
- Listen to them
- Shield them
- Let them go

Tell Them

Tell people what they need to know, including clear, well-defined goals and priorities. One of the professors explained this by saying, "If I tell you: to get an A in this course, you have to write me an excellent 10-page paper tonight. Do you think it is easier if I tell you the topic of interest to me or if I tell you to write whatever you want?" The class almost unanimously voted for the former. Research by almost all academics and management trainers has concluded that unclear or constantly shifting priorities leave employees confused, insecure, stressed, and unsatisfied.[10]

Give people effective feedback. When they are doing well, they want to be praised for it, privately and, better still, publicly. When they are not doing well, they also appreciate private constructive criticism that can help get them back on track. Whether it is positive or negative feedback, reasons and specific examples are very useful to help the recipient understand and accept the feedback. (See sidebar for things that do not help.) One of my all-time favorite books is *The One Minute Manager* by Kenneth H. Blanchard and Spencer Johnson. The book describes an effective manager as someone who gives a brief but concise praise immediately if work is well done and a brief and concise reprimand when work is not so well done. While this is a simplification, I find it a very useful reminder—to be effective, feedback should be concise, factual, non-condescending, and timely.

Ineffective Feedback

I made plenty of mistakes at giving out feedback when I first became a manager, especially in giving negative feedback. I still remember one of my biggest mistakes. . . . I was managing a team at BCG. One of the team members was new to the firm. He had a strong résumé and a great attitude. I was also flattered as he kept telling people he really liked working with me. But he kept making errors, both in crunching data and in drawing big-picture conclusions from the data. I was getting more and more frustrated. I would point out his mistakes. But instead of having any serious discussions on his poor performance, I would just say, "Do not make the mistake again. Do not get depressed. You are doing well." I kept hoping he would improve but things just got worse. He even made some grave mistakes on one of my team's final presentations, the day before we had to deliver it. His mistake resulted in the whole team—all five of us—working overnight. When the project was completed, company policy required that I gave him a formal evaluation. To be fair to the other team members, I could not help but give him a very low grade. He was furious. He said I had given him positive feedback along the way. When I tried to give him examples of his mistakes, he kept saying, "but you said I was doing well!" He asked for more examples and I could not remember the others. I have since learned to give honest and timely feedback and keep good record of facts such as examples and incidents that I will need to support the feedback.

Groom Them

Grooming includes coaching, training, and mentoring. As noted in Chapter 1, many capable people look at a paid job as an opportunity to learn instead of just an opportunity to earn a linear income. My husband once offered to double someone's salary—but the employee still resigned, saying, "Learning is more important than money." To enable people to learn effectively:

- They want both pull and push—to pick up the knowledge and skills they know they want to acquire, and also to have their superiors guide and help them on the learning process and career paths.
- They want to constantly deepen and broaden their knowledge and skill base in the areas of interest to them. They have a low boredom threshold.[11]
- They want grooming in all its different forms: formal training, on-the-job coaching, well-planned job assignments, exposure to key projects, and so on—anything that can help them learn.

Listen to Them

Everybody appreciates being listened to. Everybody appreciates having their ideas given sufficient consideration, even when the ideas are eventually rejected. It makes people feel valued. (A digression here—besides retention, listening to everyone, not just the capable and experienced staff members but even the most junior ones, can generate ideas valuable to management and business. In *How to Become a Great Boss*, Jeffrey Fox cited a true story where a leading U.S. lawyer won a major lawsuit based on a suggestion from his office cleaning lady! A law had to be changed as a result of the case!)

Shield Them

Minimize unnecessary roadblocks, especially bureaucracy, policies, and paperwork that alienate and frustrate. This seems like common sense but it is shocking how many companies are still losing talent because they throw up roadblock that people refuse to live with. Key reasons I have seen include office politics, incompetence of senior management, and failure to recognize the gravity of these issues for staff retention. Companies with such roadblocks tend to have low retention of competent staff but high retention of mediocre people who like the security of bureaucracy and paperwork or who cannot find a better working environment. (See the following sidebar for more on these problems)

Roadblocks

I once worked for a client whose CEO and chairman both adamantly proclaimed themselves leading-edge thinkers who want to build a leading-edge company with the best talent. But this is what I witnessed when I was with the company:

SHOOTING YOURSELF IN THE FOOT

The client was in the middle of changing its accounting system. This was a very important project as any loss of accounting data could lead to major business issues. The IT department was working day and night. Then one day, one of the key programmers hurt his leg really badly in a traffic accident. The doctor told him to rest at home for two months to let his leg recover. This created problems for both the company and the programmer. The company really needed his work to complete the accounting system change on time. Because two months was longer than the sick leave the programmer was entitled to, company policy required him to take unpaid leave. This would cause financial difficulties for the programmer. Also, he would be home for two months with nothing to do. His leg could not move but his mind and fingers had no problem programming.

So the programmer suggested he could work from home. It was actually more efficient for him to be programming at home as he would save a lot of commuting time and could focus better without the normal distractions in the office environment.

This would have solved the problem for everyone. Since his direct boss could monitor his output, the company could be sure that he was spending his time programming. But Human Resources vetoed the suggestion, saying "We cannot pay him a salary since we cannot monitor how much time he actually spends programming at home." I was speechless when I heard this. Why do we need to monitor the input if we get the output that is win-win to everybody?

Cutting Off Your Nose to Spite Your Face

The client owned two office buildings a few blocks from each other that it rented out for income; call them A and B. The client used a floor in building A for its own office. The car parks in both buildings were underutilized, but the one in Building B had a bigger vacancy rate because its narrow driveway made it too easy to get a car scratched. The client decided to provide parking to senior executives as a perk. This was supposed to be a win-win as it cost the company nothing but was of value to the executives. But the head of HR decided that only the board of directors should get parking in A. The rest would get parking in B, to "differentiate seniority." The result—instead of appreciating the parking space, the executives who were assigned to B resented it and became more alienated. The company was perceived as idiotic. People said, "This place is so bureaucratic that it would choose to give us parking that could scratch our cars. There are so many free spaces in A. It is also inefficient as we have to waste time to walk from B to A daily."

Getting It Right

My client offers a major contrast with some of the best practice firms. In their 20-year study of "what followers want from their leaders," Rob Goffee and Gareth Jones of London Business School found the following best practice examples on rules and policies:

- "Herb Kelleher, CEO of Southwest Airlines . . . threw the company's rule book out of the window."
- "Greg Dyke . . . when he was the director general of BBC discovered a mass of bureaucratic rules, often contradictory . . . (the rules) discourage the clever people (or high-quality staff members) on whom the reputation and future success of the BBC depended. Dyke launched an irreverent 'cut the crap' program."[12]

Let Them Go

Even if you do all four kinds of promoting measures I've described and maybe more, staff turnover is still inevitable.

I have had people resign for no other reason but desire for "a new environment to stimulate new learnings." I can do nothing to retain someone who's reached that conclusion. It is painful to lose people for reasons like that. I used to get very depressed and have had many sleepless nights from loss of key staff members. But now I have learned to keep it in perspective—the loss is painful and I will do anything I can to retain the good people, but in the end no one is irreplaceable.

HAVE A POWER TRIP

In business, everyone wants power. To have power means you can make things happen: you can make decisions that will be enforced without resistance; you can have access to information that you need to make decisions; you can allocate resources that can affect careers, job satisfaction, and remuneration, and so on.

At HBS, students take classes devoted to the topic of power. As with networking, some people are born with a talent for acquiring and using power. But for someone who (like me) lacks such natural talents, I find two discussion topics particularly useful. The first is an analytical framework to understand the sources of power. This framework can help you think through how to get power, or at least how to navigate within the power structure. The second topic is recommendations on how to start building power beyond the formal power bestowed to you by your position. Even if you run your own company and have all the power, it is important to understand both these topics, if only so you can monitor the development of your subordinates' power. This is critical to ensure that none of your subordinates is developing an inappropriate power base.

Sources of Power

At HBS, we discussed three major sources of power. The same sources are elaborated in the Harvard Business Essentials book, *Power, Influence, and Persuasion*.[13] The first is formal and can be exerted directly and forcefully. The second and the third are informal and often take the form of influence that is applied more softly.

Positional Power

This is the formal power that comes with having a position and title in the organization. Typically, the power will include managing your subordinates (work assignment, appraisal, and so on), access to certain information, inclusion in certain management meetings, and the authority to make certain decisions and mobilize certain resources.

Personal Power

This is the informal power that comes because of who you are as a person:

- Personal traits such as self-confidence, articulateness, charisma, even aggression. These traits increase your chance of getting noticed and listened to.
- Expertise such as strategic thinking, industry experience, functional knowledge, technical know-how, government relations, ability to execute, ability to generate business, and close client relationships.
- Track record of success and accomplishments.

In particular, expertise that is valued and rare in an organization can give you great power, because your opinions will be sought after and given significant weight. You can be put into leadership or advisory roles beyond your formal position. Expertise is what gives consultants their access to the ears of senior management in key positions.

Relational Power

This is another form of informal power. It comes from your relations with others in the organization. Key sources of relational power include mentorship, coalition, dependencies, and reciprocity.

Mentorship is a source of relational power. Mentors can use their relational power to influence the behavior of their protégés. I still remember many years ago when Mr. A, my mentor and my boss at BCG, asked me to take on an assignment that required stationing at a very remote area for many months. He could have used his positional power and simply told me to go. But instead, he used his relational power and said to me, "Hey Emster (a nickname he made up), will you do it for me, please? I need you there." Of course, I could not say no.

On the flip side, protégés can also leverage relational power with their mentors. I have often gone to Mr. A to ask him for information that I had no right to get—such as "am I getting a good reputation among the seniors?" I have also gone to Mr. A to get him to use his positional and other powers to help obtain high-profile assignments for me.

Being part of a coalition within the company can give you relational power. As described in *Power, Influence, and Persuasion*,[14] there are two types of coalitions: a natural coalition or a single-issue coalition. The former endure for a long time, and are developed based on shared fundamentals over a range of issues. For example, at my property investment client, the head of strategy had a natural coalition with the head of property management. Both had business school training, made decisions based on data and analysis, and were very execution-oriented. At my consumer electronics client, the marketing team, sales team, and engineering team had a shared interest to push the R&D team for faster, better, and lower-cost products. They also had a shared interest against the finance team, which was always looking for cost-cutting maneuvers. They formed a natural coalition on these issues.

Single-issue coalitions develop as parties come together for one goal. Their relational power does not extend beyond that issue. For example, many traditional Hong Kong companies work half the day on Saturdays. I have seen coalitions forming in many such companies to lobby for eliminating Saturdays as a workday. Individuals in the coalition do not have positional or personal power to lobby for the change. But appropriate coalitions can bring the issue to management's attention. Such a coalition may include many who are adversaries on other issues but are allies on this one.

Having dependents will give you relational power. Dependencies exist when your colleagues depend on you for information, services, assignments, or anything else. At my property investment client, for example, the sales VP, who was also on the Board of Directors, had very limited control over some of her general managers. The VP, for a variety of reasons, stopped focusing on getting involved with many of the tenant negotiation and relationship-building issues. She delegated most of this to her general managers. Over time, the general managers became very powerful because the VP had to depend on them for tenant relations, which was key to the rental business.

Exploiting the Law of Reciprocity can also give you significant relational power. This law was discussed in Chapter 4, in the context of networking. The better you are at giving out favors effectively, the broader and deeper relational power you have. It is like depositing into a bank account that you can draw from when you need a favor in return.

Key Steps to Build Power

The first thing to do is make sure you understand the company. When I first started doing business in Beijing, I asked a powerful mainland Chinese politician for advice on how to start developing powerful government relations in Beijing. I still remember exactly what he said: "As a newcomer to Beijing, don't do anything. The best is to read all the government news, listen, observe, and ask appropriate questions very discreetly. Meet everybody but choose your friends carefully."

I've found this advice useful—not just in a politically sensitive place like Beijing but in any new business environment. And do not wait until you first join a company; start absorbing information during your job hunt to ensure you are joining a company where you can fit. This effort should not stop until you leave the company as politics is never static.

All sources should be tapped into for as much information as possible: company annual reports, press releases, ex-employees, current employees, whoever and whatever you can find. All information is useful, especially anything that helps answer the following questions:

- *What is the formal power structure?* That is, what is the power officially vested in each key position in the organization chart? This is not confidential information and can be found relatively easily.
- *What is the informal power structure?* This could be even more important than the formal structure. What are the key decisions and projects facing the company? Who has the most influence on the decisions and projects? Who has the most personal and relational power? Who has the least? Why? What are the key mentorships, coalitions, and dependencies?
- *What is the culture of the company?* You need to know the norms, values, and ways of getting things done in the company.

Being a trained engineer and basically a straight-arrow nerd, I made plenty of mistakes in my early career because I did not appreciate the importance of understanding corporate culture. A couple of my blunders immediately come to mind:

- I was making a presentation to a Dato' in Malaysia. (*Dato'* is a rank that can be compared to the British knighthood.) He was head of the Muslim company I was consulting for. I was in the middle of presenting when the Dato' asked a question. I answered it politely but ended by saying, "but Dato', that's not the point. The point is. . . . " The whole room of client executives went absolutely quiet and all eyes turned to the Dato'. I later learned that no one in the company, especially a woman, would ever dream of speaking to the Dato' like that. I was lucky the Dato', probably seeing that I was a foreigner, decided not to fire me on the spot. But it was a close call. Ever since, I've never forgotten to pay attention to company (and country) culture.

- I was once seconded to a certain company to act as an in-house strategist. In consulting, one is trained to speak up and actively participate in meetings and in other people's presentations. Silence in meetings is often interpreted as failure to think and contribute enough. Therefore, from day one, I was very vocal in meetings. I quickly observed that everyone else, including the chief executive, was very quiet in meetings. Being an arrogant novice, I thought I was just quicker, smarter, and more articulate than everybody else there. I was feeling pretty good about myself until I got a major warning from my superior at the consulting firm. The feedback from the CEO was: "She does not listen. People are rather turned off by her constant comments and questions during meetings. She seems to have problems fitting in." Since then, I have learned to watch when not to open my mouth.

So What?

Developing a strategy to gain power has a lot of similarities to developing a strategy for a start-up. The company is your market. You need to decide your principles, values, vision, long-term strategy, and short-term tactics. These are some of the key questions to think through:

- *Does anything you know about the company power structure and culture conflict with your values or personality?* If so, this may not be the right company for you.
- *What is the future you want in the company and outside? What formal and informal power will you need to achieve your long-term goals?* For example, if you see your consulting job as the stepping-stone to finding an industry job with one of your clients, you need to gain power so as to be assigned to work with clients you might want to work for in the future.
- *What is your job now? What formal and informal power you will need to excel and learn in your job?* For example, if you are in marketing, you may need field data and insights from the sales team for your marketing plan. Hence, you will need to develop informal power over people in sales.

Based on your answers to these questions, you can start developing your road map—what power you need and how to attain it:

- *Positional power*. This kind of power is the most difficult to change, but it is not impossible. Examples I have seen: additional formal power bestowed for special projects, organizational restructuring, personnel changes, and new strategy.
- *Personal power*. This may be the easiest as many sources of personal power are skills you can choose to acquire for yourself.
- *Relational power*. Developing relational power involves third parties. This kind of power has two main categories:

  Key relationships. Naturally, focus should be on building key relationships with the people you have identified as critical to your power base. You will want to put most of your effort into creating the dependencies, extending favors, and building coalitions.

  Non-key relationships. You should not ignore people with no immediate value for your power base. Unless it would run into conflicts with key relationships or require a lot of effort, it is worth extending appropriate and easy-to-afford favors even when it is to a colleague of no apparent value to your power base.

The plan should also be one that you are comfortable in executing. Do you have the personality, capability, and determination necessary for the plan? If not, are you going to adapt yourself? Or are you going to find another company that is a better fit?

Play Your Chess

Executing the plan to attain power and then using the power is like the game of chess.

As my chess teacher always says, "You cannot become a chess champion without learning to envision the game many moves ahead." Lack of time or discipline often makes people focus too much on the present instead of thinking about future moves by others. In addition, the chess metaphor is also useful as a reminder to look at it all as a game. This can make it more interesting and easier to accept when failures (inevitably) occur.

Guard Your Reputation

Power, especially personal and relational, can be further enhanced if you develop a strong reputation based on winning traits, relationships, or track record. A strong, positive reputation can significantly increase your personal power. In the cynical but insightful book *The 48 Laws of Power*, Robert Greene and Joost Elffers explain: "So much depends on reputation—guard it with your life. . . . Through reputation alone you can intimidate and win. . . . Reputation is the cornerstone of power. . . . Your reputation inevitably precedes you, and if it inspires respect, a lot of your work is done for you."[15]

There are two ways to get a reputation: passively or actively. Passive development is the style generally used at HBS. Different people got a reputation over time: "he is really smart," "she really knows finance," "he always puts his foot in his mouth," and so on. Reputation mostly develops naturally as people interact with each other in and out of class.

Active reputation building is not taught in any HBS course, and I have not noticed anyone feeling a need to try this at HBS. But in their book, Greene and Elffers suggest you can also actively build your reputation by

- Establishing a reputation on one outstanding quality that sets you apart and gets people to notice and talk about you.
- Making your reputation known. But this has to be done subtly and with care. Overdoing it can be perceived as "bragging," "tooting your own horn," arrogant, self-centered, or egotistic.

I have seen active reputation building outside HBS, and when I notice it, it makes me more skeptical and careful about the person. For example, a few years ago, almost overnight, two unknowns became recognized by all of Hong Kong as "the richest couple in Shanghai." By combining charity donations and appearances, high-profile real estate purchases, press conferences on their businesses, and frequent sightings with socialites in Hong Kong, and be-friending socialites who then introduced them to the rich and the famous, the pair built a reputation that allowed them to attract business deals and attention from all over Hong Kong. They never publicly proclaimed them-selves "the richest couple in Shanghai," but their friends, associates, and the media constantly introduced them that way. Unfortunately, recently they were arrested for corruption. This taught me two lessons:

- What Greene and Elffers suggest does work in real life.
- Be cautious of people who have built a reputation this way.

It is interesting to point out that acquisition and exercise of personal and relational power is more or less the same as what is often referred to as "playing office politics." At HBS, many agree that, like formal power, politics is the natural by-product of human interaction. It cannot be eliminated or ignored. Understanding personal and relational power can help you decide how much politics to use and how to fit it with your own career goals and ethical standards.

Notes

1. Jim Collins, *Good to Great* (New York: HarperCollins, 2001), 13.
2. Ibid., 55.
3. Story available online: www.newworldencyclopedia.org/entry/David_Ogilvy (access date: January 17, 2009).
4. Robert Slater, *Jack Welch and the GE Way* (New York: McGraw-Hill), 41.
5. Jim Collins, *Good to Great* (New York: HarperCollins, 2001), 54–56.
6. Jeffrey J. Fox, *How to Become A Great Boss* (New York: Hyperion Books, 2002), 21.
7. Jim Collins, *Good to Great* (New York: HarperCollins, 2001), 54–56.
8. Robert Slater, *Jack Welch and the GE Way* (New York: McGraw-Hill), 38.
9. Jim Collins, *Good to Great* (New York: HarperCollins, 2001), 56.
10. Management books and research on the importance of goal setting abound. Recent books I have read include *How to become a Great Boss* by Jeffrey J. Fox, *Why Employees Don't Do What They're Supposed to Do and What to Do About It* by Ferdinand Fournies, and *First Break All the Rules* by Marcus Buckingham and Curt Coffman.
11. Rob Goffee and Gareth Jones, "Leading Clever People," *Harvard Business Review* (March 2007).
12. Ibid., 5.
13. Harvard Business Essentials, *Power, Influence, and Persuasion* (Boston: Harvard Business School Press, 2005). I find the Harvard Business Essentials series quite useful as a summary on many topics. As explained in the inside cover of each book, "the series is designed to provide comprehensive advice, personal coaching, background information, and guidance on the most relevant topics in business. . . . To ensure quality and accuracy, each volume is closely reviewed by a specialized content adviser from a world-class business school."
14. Harvard Business Essentials, *Power, Influence, and Persuasion*, (Boston: Harvard Business School Press, 2005), 20.
15. Robert Greene and Joost Elffers, *The 48 Laws of Power* (London: Profile Books, 1998), 15.

8

MARKETING

THE FANTASTIC FOUR P'S

Anyone who majored or has worked in marketing can tell you marketing is largely about successfully defining and managing Four P's: product, price, promotion, and place.

- *Product* includes tangible products and intangible services. It includes functionality, brand name, warranty, services, and accessories. In short, it is what the company is trying to charge money for.
- *Price* is what the company gets in exchange for the product. It includes pricing strategy, list price, discounts, and rebates.
- *Promotion* is communication about the product with the goal of generating positive customer response. It includes advertising, direct mail, lucky draw, public relations, and promotion budgeting.
- *Place* is distribution, that is, how to get the products to the customers. It includes wholesale and retail channel selection, order processing, warehousing, and logistics.

More detailed definitions of the Four P's can easily be found on the Internet or in any marketing textbook. HBS uses the same framework. The difference: instead of talking about definitions and theories, HBS students learn through applying the Four P's to a large number of case studies. In the following sections, I will discuss the case insights that have been most useful in helping me think about each of the Four P's.

PRODUCT: BETTER FIRST BEST?

In the United States, some brands are so successfully marketed that their name has become the generic name of a whole category. People will ask "may I have a Kleenex" instead of "may I have a tissue," and people will say "this is your Xerox copy" instead of "this is your photocopy." Other examples are Band-Aid, Jello, Q-tips, Velcro, and FedEx. In fact, I still do not know the real category name for Velcro.

While this kind of achievement (officially termed becoming a "genericized trademark") can pose significant legal issues in trademark protection, from the purely marketing product-launch perspective, these companies are often discussed at HBS as examples of great success. Analyzing the key success factors of these examples, it seems that while brands that become household words provide good products, they are not necessarily the best in their category. It is unclear and unproven that Kleenex is better than Scott, or that Xerox is better than Canon.

However, while they may or may not be the best, these successful brands were the *first product* in their category. That is, they were not necessarily the very first available in their market, but they were first to establish themselves in buyers' minds and are thus perceived as being first. In marketing, perception is often more important than reality. For example, the very first mainframe computer sold was Remington Rand but IBM became the first in the popular mind because of its massive marketing.

Being first is important because, psychologically, some people perceive the first as superior and the rest as copycats. Also, people have inertia as change usually comes with a switching cost. The time, resources, and risk of trying a new product may deter people from switching unless it offers a very compelling advantage.

The most direct way to achieve first-in-category status, of course, is to be truly the first to reach the market. For example, Xerox was indeed the first to introduce office photocopying in the 1960s.

The second way is to usurp the position through marketing. An example is IBM's victory over Remington Rand, as mentioned earlier. It must be noted that this is only possible if the market has not "made up its mind" about the category or the company. For example, once the market has made up its mind that "Kleenex" is first, it will be very difficult, if at all possible, for any company to try to take that position away from Kleenex, even with billions of marketing dollars. With the strong perception that Xerox makes copying machines, Xerox wasted decades and billions of marketing dollars and still failed to have any share in the computer market.

The third way is to try to make some variation so the category can be perceived as a new category. For example, Charles Schwab in the United States was not marketed as a new and better player in the brokerage business. It made its success by marketing itself as the first "discount" brokerage firm. The key is to identify the competitive advantage versus leading players in an established category and then try to create a new category based on this advantage. Of course, this is not always possible and is easier said than done— but it is very powerful if you can manage it.

Price: To Fight or Not to Fight

If business is like war, then price must be one of the most common, most critical, and most challenging battlefields. It is common because it is much easier to reduce price and get immediate results than to change product features, advertising, or distribution. This is true both offensively and defensively. It is critical because the stakes are high. Companies and even industries can be destroyed by price wars. An example everyone knows is the 1992 U.S. airline price war. As a result of aggressive price cuts by all major competitors, the combined losses of the industry for that year exceeded the total profits of the industry since its very beginning. Price wars are challenging because even the winner often suffers significant losses.

For these reasons, I have always paid extra attention to case discussions related to price wars. Here are the cases I have found most fascinating and valuable. They illustrate four key strategies when faced with prospects of a price war: preemption, segmentation, disguise, and retreat.

NutraSweet: Preemption

NutraSweet was a patented sweetener used in Diet Pepsi and Diet Coca-Cola. When the patent was about to expire a number of years ago, NutraSweet faced a significant threat of price pressure and possibly price war from generic sweeteners.

What would you do if you were NutraSweet? Slash price to drive competitors out of business? Advertise like crazy to build a brand? Instead of a lose-lose price war and millions of dollars of brand advertising, Nutra-Sweet cleverly preempted the price war by preparing and sharing a contingency plan with its major customers Pepsi and Coca-Cola, assuring both that it would be executed if either switched to the generic sweetener.

The plan involved a major advertising blitz that would "educate" the consumers that "the other cola" was the only one that contained NutraSweet. This was a real threat to Pepsi and Coca-Cola, given the large market at stake and the risk that consumers could be made to perceive a change in quality or taste under the influence of the advertisements. This threat was enough to deter Pepsi and Coca-Cola from considering switching, and hence the price war was preempted.

I once worked on a strategy study for a major multinational consumer electronics producer. As part of the project, I arranged an interview with the CEO of a competitor in Asia. To my surprise, the CEO himself agreed to the interview. I was even more surprised when the CEO started revealing some relatively sensitive manufacturing and cost data. Usually, for competitive interviews, we would only discuss some non-confidential market or supplier information. At the end of the interview, he said, "Do you know why I agreed to your interview and shared so much information with you? I need you to do me a favor. Bring a message to your client. Tell them we have a low cost structure. If they cut price, we will retaliate." When I passed this to my client, one of the senior executives joked, "Here is the answer to our pricing strategy!" The client was very appreciative of the information I brought back, though I never expected to be paid such high consulting fees simply to be a messenger.

FedEx: Segmentation

Imagine you are FedEx. Your key competitor, the U.S. Postal Service's Express Mail, just offered a guaranteed U.S. domestic overnight delivery by either noon or 3 PM the next day. How would you compete? Instead of competing on price, FedEx decided to offer two services: Premium and Standard. Premium would deliver by 10 AM the next day and standard by 3 PM the next day. This way, FedEx could compete with USPS on two fronts: faster service at a higher price and comparable service at a competitive price. FedEx was able to keep the higher margins from the price-insensitive customer segment and at the same time compete effectively in the lower-end market.

The FedEx case demonstrated an important concept in marketing: segmentation and target segment selection. *Segmentation* is the division of a market into groups of customers. These groups, called customer segments, have sufficiently different needs and characteristics that they can be served differently. One or more segments will then be selected as targets based on their fit with the company's strategy and its competence with the unfulfilled needs, as well as on segment profitability.

The two segments in the FedEx example are relatively easy to understand. Both groups fit FedEx's strategy of providing express service and are profitable. There were likely other segments that could have been identified—say, those that required even faster service or were willing to accept even slower service. These probably were operationally difficult to serve, strategically did not fit with FedEx, or simply were not financially attractive due to investment needs or competition.

However, many markets are much more complex than FedEx's, especially when consumers are involved. For example, I was involved in market segmentation for a tobacco company in Vietnam many years ago. The market had a proliferation of brands, and consumers made their choices based on a whole range of psychological and physical needs, including brand image, aspiration, packaging, peer pressure, tobacco content, taste, and price.

Four fundamental principles need to be understood in order to conduct more complex segmentation and target selection successfully:

- Type
- Strategy
- Selection
- Data

Type

There are two related types of segmentation:

- Based on benefits sought by customers, needs of customers, or the job they want to get done using the product or service.
- Based on observable characteristics of customers. For consumers, characteristics most often used for segmentation are demographics (such as age, sex, or income level) and psychographics (this is people's lifestyles and behaviors such the kinds of interests they have, the values they believe in, and the things they spend money or time on).

For business customers, characteristics most often used are revenue size, number of employees, industry, and geography.

The best practice is to first segment the customers based on benefits they seek. Then define key distinguishing customer characteristics for each segment so that advertising and promotions can be targeted and segment sizing can be calculated or checked. In the FedEx example, customers were segmented based on their service needs. Then, if necessary, characteristics could be defined for each segment. For example, companies in banking, legal, and consulting, of revenue size and number of employees above a certain threshold, or with an international business would probably be more likely customers for the premium service. With these characteristics defined, advertising and other efforts like direct marketing could be targeted. These characteristics would also allow FedEx to estimate the size of each segment using government, trade association, and industry statistics.

Another example of the key to first focus on need and then on characteristics is the disguised fast food restaurant example given by Professor Clayton M. Christensen and his co-authors in the *Harvard Business Review* article "Marketing Malpractice."[1] A fast-food restaurant was trying to improve sales of its milkshakes. So it segmented the frequent customers of milkshakes based on characteristics including demographics and personality. It then invited people who fit the profile to focus groups to understand their needs for the taste, texture, and price. The milkshakes were fine-tuned accordingly. However, sales did not improve.

The company then engaged in new research focused on first understanding customer needs. A new researcher spent time observing customers' purchase and consumption of the milkshakes. This researcher soon noticed a distinct segment of customers who purchased milkshakes in the morning. Interviews with these customers revealed that they purchased the shake as a light breakfast and a way to reduce boredom while driving to work. At other times of the day, the major segment was parents buying to placate their children's plea for sweets. Understanding such segmentation based on needs, the restaurant was able to fine-tune its products better. For the morning segment, it added more fruit to make the milkshakes more filling and interesting, and it instituted an express purchase process including swipe cards and dispensing machines, both of which helped to drive up sales. This segment was well-defined by the need to drive to work every day. Other characteristics such as length of drive, home location, sex, age, and so on could then be identified in order to help with promotions and advertising.

One can argue that the restaurant could have done its research in reverse. It could have first identified a segment with demographics of a certain age group living close to the restaurant but owning a car that they used to drive to work every day. This would certainly have worked too. But with so many demographic variables, it would be difficult to identify this as a distinct segment—and the original attempt to start with demographics did fail to identify this segment.

Strategy

It is important to segment according to the company's strategy. In the FedEx example, the overall strategy is to provide speedy delivery at an affordable price. Therefore, it is appropriate to segment based on need for different shipment speeds. By contrast, the Miller Lite "Catfight" advertising campaign provides a vivid example of segmentation not anchored by strategy. The strategy of the company was to increase sales, including switching drinkers of light beer from competitor Bud Lite. Market research identified the segment of young males and it was decided this segment would enjoy advertising featuring mud-wrestling supermodels. The company launched such a campaign, which attracted major viewership and market attention, including from the target segment. But sales did not increase. It was later discovered that while the target enjoyed the "Catfight" type advertising, the pleasure didn't induce many of them to switch brands.

Selection

It's necessary to understand segment attractiveness; that is, segmentation is a means to an end. For most companies, the ultimate goal is to select a segment or segments that can maximize the company's profit. The key factors to consider in this selection are the firm's ability to serve each segment, along with the competitive landscape and the profitability of each segment.

For a firm's ability to serve various segments and assess the competitive landscape, the HBS Module Note "Market Segmentation, Target Market Selection, and Positioning" suggests using the framework shown in Exhibit 8.1 to analyze each segment of the market.[2]

Each blank cell in the matrix will be a rating (either a moon chart pictogram like the ones described in Chapter 3 or a number on a five- or 10-point rating scale). The rating should be based on detailed analysis.

The five rows are the five general areas that should be considered for target selection. Each of five general areas can be eliminated or further broken

Exhibit 8.1 Market Segmentation Grid

Five General Areas	Own Company	Competitor 1	Competitor 2	. . . .
Ability to conceive and design				
Ability to produce (quality and quantity)				
Ability to market				
Ability to finance				
Ability to manage and execute				

down into subareas depending on the market. For example, for FedEx, ability to conceive and design may not be an important factor. Ability to produce may be broken down into different parts of the production process, including order taking, package pickup, and customs clearance. Then FedEx and key competitors will be rated for each of the general areas or subareas. It should be noted that too many subareas will lead to loss of focus and difficulty in making decisions. Hence this matrix should focus on the most critical success factors relevant to target segment selection. The other less critical factors can be put on another matrix for subsequent consideration.

Profitability of each segment must also be estimated. Without a good understanding of the segment profitability, companies may end up targeting and serving a low-profit or even unprofitable segment. For example, I once consulted for a bank in Indonesia whose strategy was to grow non-interest income from selling more sophisticated products and from transaction fees. The bank had a sizable wealth management business. Traditionally, it segmented the wealth management customers into platinum, gold, and silver status based on the total assets (savings, stocks and bonds, and so on) entrusted to the bank. Most of the bank's resources for product development, service, and promotions were devoted to the platinum segment, which had the most assets at the bank. However, subsequent detailed analyses showed that many platinum customers were not particularly profitable for the bank, as they were retired individuals with stable holdings in cash and stocks and did not buy new products from the bank. On the other hand, some of the silver customers were young professionals with sophisticated and significant product needs, leading to higher non-interest income for the bank. This sub-segment was highly profitable, had long-term growth potential, and fitted well with the bank's strategy. But lack of understanding of segment profitability had led to misallocation of bank's resources and under-servicing of this sub-segment.

Understanding profitability includes estimating the segment size, profit margins, and growth potential. Key sources of information will be internal company data, government and other industry statistics, and estimation. For example, for FedEx, the margins of premium service could be estimated through internal accounting data. The current and future number of companies that would require such service could be estimated based on characteristics and statistics available from other sources. The average number of packages, their destination, and growth potential for this segment could be estimated based on historical customer data and customer interviews. The estimation technique would be similar to the quantification techniques described in Chapter 12.

Data

Expect significant data collection, analysis, and iteration. To determine needs, characteristics, competitive landscape, and profitability, you will need large volumes of data and substantial analysis. Some of the tools are similar to the ones described in Part III. Others are more specific to marketing, such as customer questionnaires, focus groups, and conjoint analysis.[3] HBS does not go into technical details of these mechanisms. In my experience, it is usually more time- and cost-effective to hire market research companies to apply these tools, as they have access to teams of part-time questionnaire conductors, large databases of potential focus group participants, experienced focus group leaders and data analysis experts, and so on. But market research companies should be seen as the arms and legs, not the brains of the project. The choice of data to gather and possible segmentation of the customers should be led by company personnel or by consultants who know the company, its business, its strategy, and its operations well.

To conclude, segmentation may be easy in theory but it tends to be tough in practice. There are many ways to segment a market. Significant resources and experience are often needed to identify an effective segmentation. It takes strategic and creative thinking. It also takes a lot of patience as iteration and re-work (such as another round of questionnaires or focus groups) may be necessary.

3M: New Brand

In FedEx's case, both premium and standard services fit well with the FedEx brand. But sometimes a company may need to introduce a new brand to fight the war. This is especially true if the original brand has a premium image. An example is 3M. Back in the early 1990s, competitor Kao Corporation introduced a low-priced diskette. Despite the need to answer, 3M was reluctant to drop the prices on the 3M brand as it knew very well that a customer segment was perfectly willing to pay the higher price for the quality that 3M represented. As a result, 3M introduced a new brand called Highland to fight Kao.

Consumer Products: Kill the Competition Before It Kills You

The *Harvard Business Review* article "How to Fight a Price War" describes a very impressive episode.[4] The authors did not name the company, and though I have heard of the same case from various business school friends, no one has been able to tell me the real identity of the company or the product.

As the story goes, a major consumer products company was faced with an aggressive price-cutting competitor. The company defended itself by dropping the price of its economy-size product with a "buy one, get one free" offer. Because each unit of the economy-size product would last six months, the high-volume, price-sensitive customers that stocked up with the offer were off the market for almost a year. The competitor was put in a very difficult situation. It was not possible for the competitor to respond quickly given the stock levels, logistics, and so on. Even if it managed to respond with a similar offer, its margins would be severely affected. It also would not change the fact that the high-volume, price-sensitive customers would stock up and be off the market for a long time, hence severely affecting sales in the following months. This aggressive counter convinced the competitor to withdraw from the price-cutting adventure. In some similar situations for other markets, smaller competitors could be totally driven out of business.

Intel: Strategic Retreat

The four cases discussed thus far describe some of the ways to fight a price war. However, just as in real war, sometimes there is just no way to win a price war. It is lose-lose no matter how the war is fought. This is especially true when a product becomes generic with very limited differentiation. In such cases, some companies will choose to withdraw from the market altogether. Naturally, this is only possible if the company has other product lines or is able to constantly innovate. A key example is Intel. Intel stopped making DRAM chips and focused on other products when price pressure from Asian manufacturers on DRAM intensified. Another example is 3M, which exited from the videotape business when videotapes became a generic product offered by many low-priced manufacturers.

PROMOTION: WHERE IS THE MONEY?

Promotion includes above-the-line and below-the-line marketing. *Above-the-line marketing* uses mass media such as television, radio, newspapers, Internet banners, and the like. *Below-the-line* usually focuses on more direct means, such as direct paper mail or e-mail, flyers, coupons, gift with purchase, and lucky draws.

I am a naturally cost-conscious person. Hence, though I believe promotion is an essential part of marketing, I want to be sure that the money is spent wisely. When examining effectiveness of promotional spending, my education and experience tell me to adhere to three fundamental principles:

- Brands cannot live on advertising alone
- Find the "monopoly window"
- Understand promotion profitability

Brands Cannot Live on Advertising Alone

Advertising is important. It is the fastest way to reach a large audience. But advertising is not omnipotent. It is expensive and risky to rely on advertising alone to build a brand. As Professor Clayton M. Christensen of HBS and his coauthors clearly stated in the *Harvard Business Review* article "Marketing Malpractice": "advertising alone cannot build a brand, but it can tell people about an existing branded product's ability to do a job well (fulfill a need)."[5] Here are two examples to help illustrate this point:

- *Unilever Soupy Snax—4:00.* Through market research, Unilever discovered a need in the office worker segment for an afternoon snack. Many office workers who got tired around 4 PM were using caffeinated beverages, junk food, or short breaks to reenergize. So Unilever introduced Soupy Snax—4:00, a nutritious soup that was easy to heat up in the office pantry. To market this product, Unilever launched an advertisement featuring drained office workers perking up after drinking Soupy Snax—4:00.[6]

- *Miller Lite Catfight.* As discussed in the section on segmentation, through market research, Miller Lite identified the segment of young male that would enjoy advertising featuring mud-wrestling super-models. Hence, they launched the "Catfight" advertising campaign.

The Soupy Snax campaign was a major success resulting in high sales. The "Catfight" got a lot of attention from media and consumers but failed to increase sales. One key difference: in the first one, advertising was used to highlight an unsatisfied need and how the product could fulfill that need. The second one was creative and entertaining but did nothing to convince consumers to switch.

I do not have the research data to say that no brand can succeed on advertising alone, and it's hard to prove a negative anyway. Probably some have. But being of a cost-conscious turn of mind, I would prefer to maximize the chance of success by ensuring that advertising is used in a supporting role, not the lead role.

Find the "Monopoly Window"

The U.S. motor industry has always been highly competitive, with a handful of major players. The industry provides a lot of interesting case examples in many areas, including below-the-line promotions. Two well-known ones:

- In 2005, GM implemented a high-profile "you pay what we (employees) pay" promotion. In this promotion, customers were offered the "staff price," which was a deep discount from the regular retail price.
- In the same year, the Pontiac division of GM sponsored an episode of the TV reality show *The Apprentice* where competing teams were given the task of producing a brochure for the limited edition 2006 Pontiac Solstice. The episode showed how the teams designed the brochure and, of course, the distinguishing features of Solstice were highlighted. Viewers were pointed to Yahoo for additional information and a "chance" to order a unit of the limited edition.

The results of the two promotions were vastly different. For the employee-discount offer, competitors retaliated with major price cuts. The resulting bloodbath cost GM and its competitors billions of dollars.

Meanwhile, the TV show was a major success. The target was to sell 1,000 cars in 10 days. All 1,000 were sold in less than an hour.

The key differences between these two efforts highlight a number of best practices in designing promotions:

- Avoid promotions that just mask price reductions. Saying "you pay what we pay" is a price reduction. It is not even well-disguised. Some other schemes such as double loyalty points are price reductions in a slightly better disguise. However, competitors and customers both see through such ploys quickly. This can result in tit-for-tat reductions from competitors, that is, a price war—which is lose-lose. Such tactics can also inspire customers who would otherwise have paid full price to load up on extra inventory for future use (called "forward buying") so that not only do they not pay full price now, they don't pay it for a long time to come either.
- Invest creative and organizational resources to maximize the "monopoly window." This is a term originated in the MIT *Sloan Management Review* article "A Strategic Perspective on Sales Promotions."[7] In the article, Professor Betsy Gelb and coauthors Demetra Andrews and Son K. Lam defined "monopoly window" as the time between the point where customers start making purchases driven by the promotion and the time competitors launch their defenses. Figure 8.1 illustrates the concept.

In other words, the period between the time customers start to respond to the promotion and competitors can react will be the window where the company's promotion can "monopolize" the market with the offer available to the customers. The bigger the monopoly window, the greater the chance of

Figure 8.1 The Monopoly Window

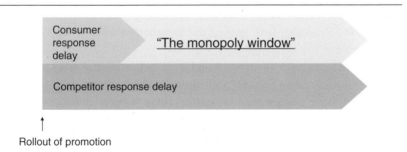

Source: Betsy Gelb, Demetra Andrews, and Son K. Lam, "A Strategic Perspective on Sales Promotions," *MIT Sloan Management Review* 48, no. 4 (Summer 2007): 3.

the promotion being a success. The window can be maximized by speeding up customer response or delaying competitors' response. In the case of the Pontiac Solstice, customer response was sped up by leveraging a popular TV program, immediate Internet access for information, and the "ticking clock" of a limited edition. Competitors simply could not respond—it would take a new product ready to launch and a lot of time to figure out a countermove.

A long monopoly window does not happen by chance. It takes ingenuity, creativity, competitive savvy, marketing expertise, discipline, stealth negotiations, and well-coordinated execution.

Understand Promotion Profitability

It is surprising how many companies do not rigorously analyze the profitability of their promotions. I once had a liquor client that measured promotion profitability by the total number of cases sold during the promotion. The fact that each case was sold at a discount price and that a lot of the sales reflected forward buying (customers stocking up for future use rather than really increasing consumption) was ignored. And I worked for a property investment firm that owned a high-end shopping mall. The mall had a very active promotion calendar with promotions such as free parking, gift with purchase, and other maneuvers. But the profitability of all these promotions was never measured because it was, according to the head of sales and marketing, "too difficult to quantify."

It is critical to measure profitability and to measure it correctly. Between 1982 and 1990, Professor Leonard M. Lodish and Magid M. Abraham studied promotions of all brands in 65 product categories in the United States and found that only 16 percent were profitable![8] I helped my liquor and shopping mall clients make some rough assessments of their promotion profitability. The analysis found that the former was losing money from many of its promotions and more than half of the promotions done by the latter were unprofitable.

The key in measuring promotion profitability is to focus on incremental profit. *Incremental profit* is what the company makes above and beyond what would have been made without the promotion. There are two categories of profit that would have been made without promotion:

- Baseline profit: Profits from purchases that customers would have made at full price without any promotion. With the promotion, this same volume is purchased at a discount price.

- Forward buying profit: Profits from purchases the customers would have made at full price in a later period without the promotion. With the promotion, customers buy the same volume at a discount price earlier and stock up for future use.

The reduction from what that would have been made if baseline and forward buying purchases had been at full price must be taken into account when assessing promotion profitability.

Table 8.1 is an example of a framework to estimate incremental profit using disguised data from my liquor client, which sells to retailers. Assume the liquor costs $40 a case to produce (cost of goods), sells at $100 a case without promotion, and is promoted at a 10 percent discount for a month. Assume $5,000 for the cost of planning and execution of the promotion, including advertising and printing of promotion materials, human resources, allocated overhead, and other details.

This framework can be used to assess a promotion after it is finished, and it can be applied in the planning stage with "target volume to be sold" replacing actual "volume sold" during the promotion period. But whether it is

Table 8.1 Estimating Incremental Profit

1. Total volume sold during promotion period	2,000 cases
2. Estimated baseline volume	900 cases
3. Estimated forward buying volume	300 cases
4. Estimated incremental volume	$2,000 - 900 - 300 = 800$ cases
5. Revenues from incremental volume	$800 \text{ cases} \times \$90 = \$72,000$
6. Manufacturing cost (cost of goods sold) of incremental volume	$800 \text{ cases} \times \$40 = \$32,000$
7. Loss of revenues due to discount	$(900 + 300) \text{ cases} \times \$10 = \$12,000$
8. Other costs of promotion	$5,000
9. Total cost of the promotion	$\$32,000 + \$12,000 + \$5,000 = \$49,000$
10. Profit from the promotion	$\$72,000 - \$49,000 = \$23,000$

for post-promotion assessment or for planning, the challenge is in estimating baseline sales and forward buying. There are two main ways to estimate these figures: you can build a systematic approach for it, or you can take your best estimate based on the data you have.

System

The most accurate way of course is to develop and apply statistical analytical algorithms. This is possible if you have accurate and timely sales data such as supermarket scanning data for consumer goods. In the study mentioned earlier, Lodish and Abraham estimated baseline sales of the 65 product categories using scanning data from supermarkets that showed purchases by consumers before, during, and after the promotion period. A detailed algorithm was developed to project baseline sales for the promotion period itself. However, even with this amount of data and analytical power, the system could not estimate the consumers' forward buying.

Best Estimate

As discussed earlier, hard data is often unavailable. Also, systems take a lot of time and resources to build and are often imperfect even if built. In such cases, best-effort estimates should be made based on historical data, market trends, sales force field input, and management judgment. In the liquor client example, we identified some smaller trade customers who were not forward buying (because they had policies against it or couldn't afford it). Trends of orders from these clients helped to estimate the baseline. For those that were forward buying, salespeople held discussions with their management to understand volume and pattern of forward buying. Sales to these clients before and after the promotion were also studied to estimate the volume of forward buying. In the end, the team of marketing and sales personnel agreed on a best estimate based on information collected. This process was difficult at first, but it became more structured and easier once people got familiar with the process. Since the numbers produced by such a process are estimates, they should be used with caution.

To help provide estimates, some mechanisms can also be implemented, either permanently or as part of each promotion. While most of these mechanisms do not provide enough accurate and detailed data for system-type analysis, they do provide invaluable data to help with getting the best estimates.

- The property investment client started to collect turnover rent, which requires retail tenants to provide them with each store's total monthly sales dollars (please see Appendix A for detailed explanation). Although not as timely and detailed as actual scanning data, monthly data are very useful in helping to analyze the effectiveness of promotions.
- The shopping mall client also started a discipline of conducting shopper questionnaires during each promotion period with such questions as "Why did you shop here today?" and "Do you find this promotion attractive?" These questionnaires were simple (with three to five questions) and conducted randomly at the mall or at gift redemption desks.
- The liquor client started including lucky draw tickets or gift redemption forms whereby it could capture consumer purchase data when the consumers sent in their tickets or forms.

If data is simply not sufficient to project baseline or forward buying figures, you can calculate them by a shortcut. The formula I use is:

G' = Gross margin $ per unit after discount (in other words, discounted price minus cost of goods sold)

V' = Total volume sold during promotion (including incremental, baseline and, forward buying)

E = Other expenses like printing and direct mail related to this promotion

G = Gross margin $ per unit without promotion discount

V = Total volume that would have been sold without discount (including baseline and forward buying)

For a promotion to be profitable:

$$(G'^{*}V' - E) > G^{*}V$$
$$V < (G'^{*}V' - E)/G$$

$G,'$ G, and E are all known variables. V' is either the target or actual total volume, which is also a known variable. This means the right side of the equation can be turned into a number. V must be smaller than this number for the promotion to have a positive impact on company's financials. The question to ask is whether the company believes it would only be able to sell V or less without the promotion.

PLACE: WHAT IS THE MAP LIKE?

Before a decision can be made on where to distribute, a thorough understanding of the market is necessary. I have found two tools particularly useful as a first step to understanding distribution of any market: a channel map and a cost structure calculation.

Basic Channel Map

A channel map displays how products are distributed and the importance of each channel. Figure 8.2 is an example from my liquor client (data is disguised).

A few points are worth noting on channel maps. The percentages on the maps can be drawn based on volume or value of goods depending on market characteristics and data availability. The idea is to show the relative importance of the channels. Make sure that the percentages add up to 100 percent, so you're looking at the whole picture.

Draw a few channel maps to help you brainstorm and to highlight any issues. This includes a map for the whole market, for key competitors, and for the company itself. These maps should then be compared and the similarities and differences should be identified and assessed.

For markets where channels have been changing or are changing, it may also be valuable to project the future channel map. For example, for the liquor client, imagine that Internet sales are expected to grow much faster than the other channels. Then by estimating the growth rate of each channel and then applying the growth rate on the current map, the future map can be drawn to

Figure 8.2 An Example of a Channel Map

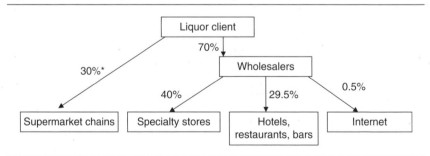

* All percentages are based on volume, not value.

assess the importance of the new channel and to stimulate discussions on channel strategy.

Figure 8.2 is just an example of the format of a map. The format can be adapted based on the situation. For example, sometimes it may be possible to draw the different boxes of the distribution map proportional to the importance of the channel. Alternatively, if you're working with a manufacturer who sells directly to retailers with no middleman, you may want to display the information in a format like the one shown in Figure 8.3, so you can also see the margins from each channel.

The key is to creatively design a map that displays the data in a format useful for analysis, discussion, and decision making.

Data for these maps can come from similar sources to the ones used for quantitative data for strategy study: government statistics, trade journals, internal experts, and supplier and customer interviews.

Cost Structure

In addition to channel maps, understanding distribution cost is also critical in any distribution plans. This includes two aspects of distribution cost: the

Figure 8.3 A Channel Map with Margins

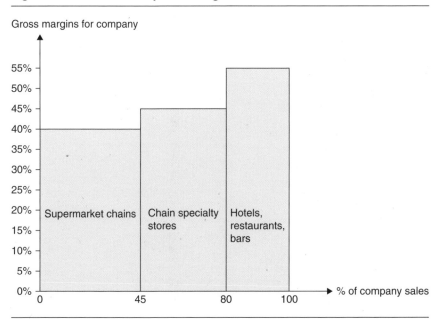

impact of total distribution cost on total company cost and the relative cost of serving different channels. As an example, Figure 8.4 is the distribution cost breakdown for the music industry, where distribution cost represents a major cost of the product.

In Figure 8.4, the retailer margin is not unusually high. It is important to understand distributors' (wholesalers, agents, retailers) margins. The margins should be studied together with the value-added by the distributor. High margins but replaceable value-added means there may be an opportunity for a more cost-effective distribution strategy, or even *disintermediation* (going direct and by-passing the distributor).

If the cost of different channels is very different, it is worth doing a cost breakdown for each channel. For example, if selling music CDs through major department stores has a different cost structure (different manufacturer margins due to different price points, different amount of sales staff time, and so on) than selling through specialty stores, then it will be worth doing the cost breakdown shown above for each of the channels.

Figure 8.4 Cost Breakdown for a Compact Disc

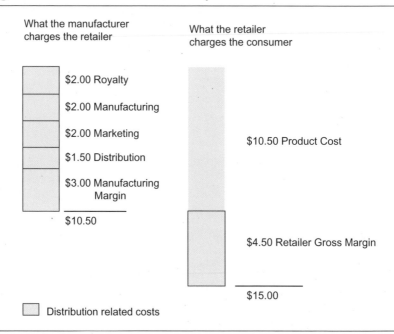

What the manufacturer charges the retailer

What the retailer charges the consumer

$2.00 Royalty

$2.00 Manufacturing

$2.00 Marketing

$1.50 Distribution

$3.00 Manufacturing Margin

$10.50

$10.50 Product Cost

$4.50 Retailer Gross Margin

$15.00

☐ Distribution related costs

Source: Nirmalya Kumar, "From Declining to Growing Distribution Channels," *Harvard Business Review*, March 2005, Figure 4.3.

When used together, the channel map and the cost structure can provide some basic information as the first step to identifying the key channels that best fit with the company's strategy and target end users.

Notes

1. Clayton M. Christensen, Scott Cook, and Taddy Hall, "Marketing Malpractice: The Cause and the Cure," *Harvard Business Review* (December 2005).
2. Miklos Sarvary and Anita Elberse, "Market Segmentation, Target Market Selection and Positioning," *Harvard Business School Module Note* (Boston: Harvard Business School Press, April 2006). Module notes are written to provide HBS students with basic knowledge in selected areas.
3. *Conjoint analysis* is a rather widely used statistical technique used in market research to determine how consumers value different features of a product or service.
4. Akshay R. Rao, Mark E. Berge, and Scott Davis, "How to Fight a Price War," *Harvard Business Review*, (March–April 2000).
5. Clayton M. Christensen, Scott Cook, and Taddy Hall, "Marketing Malpractice: The Cause and the Cure," *Harvard Business Review* (December 2005).
6. Ibid.
7. Betsy Gelb, Demetra Andrews, and Son K. Lam, "A Strategic Perspective on Sales Promotions," *MIT Sloan Management Review*, Summer 2007.
8. Magid M. Abraham and Leonard M. Lodish, "Getting the Most Out of Advertising and Promotion," *Harvard Business Review* (May–June 1990).

9

SALES

PEOPLE: BORN OR MADE, OR BOTH?

No classic, well-known, well-accepted framework for sales is comparable to the powerful Four P's marketing framework. Trying to come up with the key tools in sales, I realized, by pure coincidence, that they can be summarized into my own four P's for sales: people, perspective, process, and performance management.

People first. While all functions depend on good people, sales seem to be the one that relies on people most. Salespeople are the key point of contact between the company and its most important constituents, its customers. Everyday experience and academic research both indicate certain inherent, generic personality traits, such as *empathy* (ability to treat customers' problems as their own) and *ego drive* (ability to persist even after experiencing failure) make some people naturally better at sales than others.[1] Sports is a good analogy here—although everyone can try to play, some people have the speed, bone structure, or determination that make them naturally more suited for sports.

However, this does not mean people with one specific set of personality traits can excel at any sales job. Different categories of sales jobs will require different mixes of personality traits. Using the sports analogy again—while people with speed, sturdy bones, and determination are generally good at sports, the requirements for football will be very different from those for gymnastics. In the *Harvard Business Review* article "Comparing HBS MBAs with Top Hunter and Farmer Sales Reps," the authors explained that there are at least two different kinds of sales jobs:

- *Hunters.* This is where salespeople have to source new leads and secure new business. This kind of sales job requires people with strong initiative to identify and follow-up on new leads, persuasiveness to "get a foot in the door," and ego drive to bounce back from frequent rejections.
- *Farmers.* This is where salespeople have to maintain long-term relationships with recurring customers and get new business largely through customer referrals. This kind of sales job requires empathy and the ability to develop long-term relationships.

People who fit well with one kind of sales job may not fit at all with the other kind. This becomes especially apparent when a company is making or in need of making a transition. For my property investment clients, for example, the decades before 1997 saw a booming suppliers' market. Commercial and retail tenants were lining up to fill the client's retail and commercial properties. The 1997 Asian financial crisis turned real estate rentals into a buyers' market. The sales force, made up mostly of farmers, had difficulty getting new tenants. They did not even know how to start—how to come up with a target list and how to make a cold call. They also were not used to the rejection inevitable with cold calling. As a result, the sales manager and many members of the sales team eventually had to be replaced. As another example, in late 2007 and early 2008, Alibaba Group announced that it would reorganize its sales force into two main groups, "hunters" and "farmers." Despite the immediate negative impact on revenues since salespeople had to spend time training for the reorganization rather than selling, the company believed this move was important to its longer-term competitiveness.

PERSPECTIVE: DON'T LOSE IT

Sometimes even the most talented sales rep can lose perspective. Perspective is critical to ensure focus and priorities. This section discusses the key perspectives I learned from HBS:

- Sell benefits, not products.
- Put words in their mouths.

- You are not there to eat, drink, and be merry.
- Angry customers—if they don't kill you, they will make you stronger.

Sell Benefits, Not Products

The great Harvard professor Theodore Levitt used to tell HBS students, "People don't want to buy a quarter-inch drill. They want a quarter-inch hole!" This quote is often mentioned in classes and among students to remind us to keep perspective when selling (and marketing). While it may seem like a simple concept, it is easy for salespeople or even companies to lose track of, as explained by Professor Steenburgh of HBS: "While it may seem obvious that time should be spent trying to anticipate customers' needs, many firms give training only on product features, not on customer benefits."[2]

Jeffery Fox, HBS MBA graduate and best-selling author, goes one step further, advising us to not just sell benefits, but sell quantified benefits. In *How to Become a Rainmaker*, he writes, "Rainmakers (successful high-level salespeople) help the customer see the money. Rainmakers turn benefits into dollars."[3] This is especially true when selling new products or big-ticket items to companies. I found that while it is often difficult to quantify with perfect accuracy, the logic and analytics for quantification are already very helpful to both the prospect and me. The exercise helps convince prospects that I understand their business and can think in their position (empathy). The exercise also helps enforce a discipline on me to understand the details of what I am selling.

Put Words in Their Mouths

Once the benefits for the prospect are obvious to the sales rep, the temptation is to go on and on to explain them to the prospect. But it must be remembered that people tend to take ownership of their own ideas more firmly than when they have to champion other people's ideas. In the same HBS module note mentioned earlier, Professor Steenburg teaches HBS students: "A critical component . . . is that the prospect feels that they participated in defining the benefits that would be attained or, better still, that they defined them on their own. This leads to stronger commitment and a sense of urgency to complete the purchase. It also increases the prospect's willingness to 'sell' the product to others in the decision making unit."[4]

You Are Not There to Eat, Drink, and Be Merry

To maximize time for business and to be able to speak in a more relaxed manner, it is now very common to have business breakfast, business lunch, business golf, and so on. It is important to keep in mind that these are *business* meetings and sales calls. The focus is selling, not the daily specials at the restaurant or the golf score. Take a business lunch for example. I have learned to eat a snack and have my coffee before I go so I don't suffer hunger or caffeine-withdrawal pangs. When I am there, I order one course only unless the prospect insists I order more. This is to minimize interruptions from waiters. I order something I can eat easily, like shell pasta, soup, or a rice dish so I won't be prevented from talking because my mouth is full or I have to chew for a long time before swallowing. I never order deep-colored food like eggplant that can be conspicuously caught between my teeth without my knowing. I never order messy food like burgers or spaghetti that can easily spill on me. I like food that I can easily eat with one hand, like soup or risotto, as this can free up my right hand if I need to write. This is all common sense. As long as you keep the perspective that business comes first, it is easy to figure out the other details.

Angry Customers—If They Don't Kill You, They Will Make You Stronger

Management guru Tom Peters writes on his Web site, "There's nothing cooler than an angry customer! The most loyal customers are ones who had a problem with us . . . and then marveled when we went the Extra Ten Miles to fix it! Business opportunity No. 1 = Irate customers converted into fans."[5] You will understand how this works if you have been very mad but a salesperson managed to solve your problem beyond your expectation.

PROCESS: MAKE ANYONE A BETTER SALES REP

As Professor Thomas Steenburgh explains in the HBS module note "Personal Selling and Sales Management": "Some people are better suited to selling than others . . . and yet most people can sell more effectively by learning to follow a process."[6]

As noted earlier, to me, process includes not just defined procedures but automation and tools that can support the process. Many key strategic and managerial issues in sales can be much better addressed using a more scientific, process-oriented approach. One such issue is resource allocation, as discussed for "Company P" in Chapter 6.

Once a process is developed to allocate sales resources to the most attractive customer segments and accounts, another area that can be improved by a similar approach is the selling process. The selling process includes pre-sale preparation, actual selling, and post-purchase service. Each of these steps can be made more effective by a disciplined, defined process supported by automation and tools. For example, for pre-sale, a systematic procedure can be set up whereby the sales team is required to follow a defined checklist to prepare for each sales call (see sidebar). Another tool useful for pre-sale is systematic data and information. For example, SAP Americas (a major U.S. software company) is well-known for regularly informing its sales force of which SAP products can be most valuable to the target customer segment based on latest industry trends.[7]

An example for effective post-purchasing service process is FedEx: the package pickup and delivery process is clearly defined and handheld computers help track it for each package.

Sample Pre-Sale (or Pre-Sales-Call) Checklist

☐ Written sales call objective
☐ Needs analysis questions to ask
☐ Something to show
☐ Anticipated customer concerns and objections
☐ Points of difference from competitors
☐ Meaningful benefits to customers
☐ Dollarized approach: investment return analysis
☐ Strategies to handle objections and eliminate customer concerns
☐ Closing strategies
☐ Expected surprises

This list is very broad. Each of the items on the list can be made more detailed, with further guidelines, rules, best practice, and so on to provide salespeople with a more structured, guided approach.

Source: Jeffrey J. Fox, *How to Become a Rainmaker* (New York: Hyperion, 2000), 16–17.

Performance Management: Measure Top, Bottom, Backward, Forward . . . All Directions

What gets measured gets done. Performance management, including the setting of sales targets and performance measures and the monitoring of performance, is especially important for the sales function for the obvious reason that performance of the sales function makes a direct impact on the company's financials. Sales targets that are too high or too low can demoralize or demotivate. Performance measures that focus solely on sales achieved will mean, as Bill McDermott, president and CEO of SAP Americas, explains, "You're missing the most important element, which is the future."[8] Some of the best practices in performance management are target setting and measurement by balanced scorecard and pipeline analysis.

Target Setting: Top Down and Bottom Up

I once had a multinational client who commissioned a major global consulting study to find the optimal way of doing its annual plan, especially the budget part of the plan. More than 20 leading multinationals were interviewed. The simplified skeleton of the recommendation is given in Figure 9.1.

Figure 9.1 Best Practice Target-Setting Process

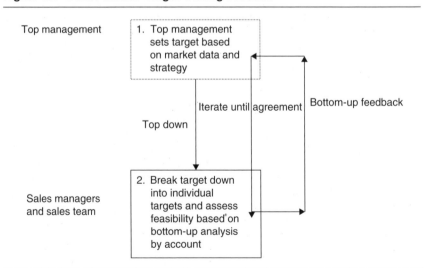

In the *Harvard Business Review* article "The New Science of Sales Force Productivity," the authors described how adoption of a similar process at Aggreko North America, a division of U.K.-based equipment rental company Aggreko, led to a 29 percent of increase in sales and 90 percent increase in sales force productivity within one year![9]

Performance Measurement: Balanced Scorecard and Pipeline Analysis

The Balanced Scorecard framework (discussed in more detail in Part III) can be applied effectively to the sales function. Among the measures for sales, the one I have found especially useful is pipeline targets. For example, CEO Bill McDermott set a pipeline standard whereby his salespeople were expected to have three times their annual sales quotas in their pipeline of prospects. The target for pipeline is usually determined by estimating the conversion rate. That is, if you expect 10 percent success rate, then you should have 10 prospects in the pipeline for every sale you expect to make.

Notes

1. David Mayer and Herbert M. Greenberg, "What Makes a Good Salesman," *Harvard Business Review* 42, no. 4 (2006): 119–125.
2. Thomas Steenburgh, "Personal Selling and Sales Management" (Module note), (Boston: Harvard Business School Press, December 2006). Module notes are prepared for the purpose of aiding students in specific knowledge area.
3. Jeffrey Fox, *How to Become a Rainmaker* (New York: Hyperion, 2000).
4. Thomas Steenburgh, "Personal Selling and Sales Management" (Module note), (Boston: Harvard Business School Press, December 2006). Module notes are prepared for the purpose of aiding students in specific knowledge area.
5. Tom Peters, "Wherefore The Impact Of Superior Management Practice on Increased Human Welfare and the Pursuit of Happiness* and Excellence?" n.d., p. 22. Available online: www.tompeters.com/blogs/freestuff/uploads/ TP_Purpose083107.pdf (access date: January 18, 2009).
6. Thomas Steenburgh, "Personal Selling and Sales Management" (Module note), (Boston: Harvard Business School Press, December 2006). Module notes are prepared for the purpose of aiding students in specific knowledge area.
7. Dianne Ledingham, Mark Kovac, and Heidi Locke Simon, "The New Science of Sales Force Productivity," *Harvard Business Review* (September 2006): 124–133.
8. Ibid.
9. Ibid.

10

FINANCE

PROFIT IS NOT CASH

One of the most fundamental concepts in finance is "cash is king." Most people find income statements intuitive. Sales minus cost equals profit; what could be simpler? Hence many people think about starting, investing in, or running a "profitable business" where profit (the bottom line) is attractive. However, few realize the difference between profit and cash, and often realization comes only when they are trapped in a cash crunch. (If you have experienced cash crunches before and can understand very well why it is critical to monitor and plan cash flow rather than profit, you can skip this chapter. You already know the key principles.)

If you are unsure why cash is key, take a look at the examples in Tables 10.1 and 10.2. It is an exaggerated example to illustrate the importance of looking at cash rather than profit.

The company had no sales last year because it was being set up, but the projection for the current year is 100 percent guaranteed. Would you buy Y at US$100,000? It looks like it cannot be that Table 10.1 shows how you can make your money back within the year!

But would it make a difference if you were to learn the following tidbits:

- Instead of the normal 30- or 60-day credit terms, Y gives customers 13-month credit terms. This means US$1 million revenues will be collected next year, not the current year.

149

Table 10.1 Projected Profits

	Company Y Annual Profit and Loss for the Current Year (US$)
Revenues	1,000,000
Costs of goods sold	400,000
Salary, rent, other expenses	300,000
Net Profit	300,000

- Unfortunately, Y's suppliers, employees, landlords, and other debtors are not as lenient. They all need to be paid 30 days after goods are delivered (suppliers), at the end of the month (employees), or even at the beginning of the month (rent).

Now what? All of a sudden, the financials are changed. Your cash flow projections for the year will look like Table 10.2.

So, you won't just need US$100,000 to purchase the company, you also have to have US$700,000 cash to operate the business in the first year! You will then get the projected US$1 million in revenues after the first year. Therefore, as Harold Williams, the former chairman of the Securities and Exchange Commission, commented in *Forbes*, "If I had to make a forced choice between having earnings information and having cash flow information . . . I would take cash flow information."[1]

Table 10.2 Projected Cash Flow

	Company Y Cash Flow for the Current Year (US$)
Revenues collected	0
Costs of goods sold	400,000
Salary, rent, other expenses	300,000
Net Profit	−700,000

Profit is an abstract entity. Profit is not tangible. You cannot touch or count profit. You cannot pay your bills with profit. Only cash is real. Your suppliers will gladly accept your cash—but not your profit. In one extreme case I saw, one of my clients sold his products to a company that subsequently went bankrupt. The company was profitable on paper. However, to push sales, the company's management gave its customers a 24-month installment payment plan. To make it worse, no one at the company was following up with the customers to collect. Salespeople considered their jobs done once a sale was made. Also, since maintaining a good relationship with customers was important, salespeople did not see any benefit in pushing for on-time payment. On the other hand, finance department was mostly made up of clerks and bookkeepers. They were very diligent and accurate in recording payments when the payments arrived but they did not see getting the payments in the first place as their responsibility. Unfortunately the bank was not as "disorganized" as my client was. My client's company was forced into bankruptcy after it defaulted on a few payments owed to the bank.

In the same way, the more time you get before you actually have to pay your expenses, the better it is for your cash flow. It is well-known that the travel agency business in Hong Kong has very thin margins. I was told that in some cases an agent makes only US$2 to $3 on a US$300 air ticket! So why are there still so many travel agencies? One of the reasons is cash flow. Travel agencies get you to pay prior to your trip but they often do not pay the airlines, hotels, and restaurants (for package tours) until much later. In the years before the 1997 Asian financial crisis, many travel agency owners would use the cash flow to invest in real estate. All became very rich, though many lost a significant part of their wealth after the crisis.

Let Bygones Be Bygones

Cash is king but cash that has already been spent and is largely irretrievable probably should not be considered in future decisions. This is the all-important "sunk cost" concept. Here is a trap that is easy to fall into:

- You invest in a stock and it is now making a loss. It isn't clear when (or if) the stock will rebound. Instead of selling it and redeploying the capital to other, more attractive investments, the temptation is to hold onto the stock in the hope that its price will bounce back to above the purchase level.

- Sunk cost does not always have to be about money. For example, suppose you've already spent days reading this book and you are almost finished. You have found it boring and have not learned anything from it. Looking at the table of contents, none of the remaining topics really interests you. But instead of putting the book away and reading another book that may be more interesting, you figure maybe you should finish reading this one since you "have read so much already . . . may as well finish it."

Many people fail to apply sunk cost when they are making decisions. There are a variety of reasons for this:

- *Lack of experience or training.* As a result, they fail to quickly recognize what is sunk cost and what is not.
- *Loss aversion due to human psychology.* Whether they are conscious of it or not, most people are naturally averse to loss. This could be due to the need to save face, or to the psychological difficulty of accepting that the earlier decisions were wrong and a loss has been incurred.
- *Loss aversion due to corporate pressures or misaligned incentives.* Employees do not want to have to admit to their superiors that their decisions have led to waste. Management does not want to admit waste to shareholders. For public companies, admitting waste may mean whatever is sunk has to be taken off the current year profit (a write-off). This will also affect share price and possibly the careers of those involved.
- *Loss of objectivity.* The examples presented thus far are deliberately straightforward to illustrate the concept. But in reality, some parameters are always estimates rather than definite numbers, making it tempting to hold out. For example, if you are deciding to hold or sell stock, you have to compare the future prospects of your stock with other investment options such as other stocks or properties. The different options may have different risks, growth prospects, and so on. Hence comparing these options will involve estimation and possibly some subjective judgment. Well-known experiments by psychologists have shown that people often become more optimistic about their investments once the investments are made (see sidebar). This means that in this example, even people who understand sunk cost may be overly optimistic about the option they have invested in compared to their other options.

Loss of Objectivity on Sunk Costs

A number of well-known experiments have been conducted to show that people often inflate probability estimations on the outcome of an investment once the investment is made. One of the best-known ones was conducted by R. E. Knox and J. A. Inkster in 1968.[2] In the experiment, 141 horse bettors where studied: about half who had just finished placing a bet in the past 30 seconds and the other half just about to place a bet in the next 30 seconds. The bettors were asked to rate their expectation of their horse's chances of winning on a seven-point scale—the higher the point, the higher the expectation of the horse winning. The result—3.48 average for the people before betting and 4.81 average for the people after betting. Subsequent experiments done by Knox and Inkster and a number of other psychologists produced similar findings.[3]

Hence, it is easy for even experienced businesspeople to fall into the sunk cost trap. Sometimes, decision makers have to be replaced so an organization can avoid the sunk cost trap. In the *Harvard Business Review* article "The Hidden Traps in Decision Making," the authors cited a real-life example:

> One of us helped a major U.S. bank discover that bankers responsible for originating the problem loans were far more likely to advance additional funds—repeatedly, in many cases—than were bankers who took over the accounts after the original loans were made . . . . had tried, consciously or unconsciously, to protect their earlier, flawed decisions. They have fallen victim to the sunk-cost bias. The bank finally solved the problem by instituting a policy requiring that a loan be immediately reassigned to another banker as soon as any problem arose.[4]

ASK, NICELY

For most companies, regular financial statements including the income statement, balance sheet, and cash flow statement are generated regularly by accounting staff using accounting software. Key measures can be read off or calculated from these statements based on definitions approved by authorities (accounting rules, tax laws, rating agency guidelines) and by management.

To explain the construction of financial statements and all the possible key measures that can be derived from the statements is beyond the scope of this book. They are not difficult, just full of details. (A slight digression here: I strongly advise that anyone interested in business should take at least a course in accounting. I had one course in accounting during my under-graduate days at Stanford. The key principles I learned there have served me well even to this day. A degree or an accreditation in accounting would have been even better, even for someone who does not want to be an accountant. Besides in-depth knowledge that is useful in management, such qualification can also open the path to a career as a CFO, which could be another way toward becoming a CEO. Without the academic qualification, such a career path is not even an option.) HBS does not teach details of how to prepare financial statements. Such data is usually already provided in the case studies. It is assumed that in real life, these statements would be prepared by qualified accounting personnel. Therefore, the focus at HBS is on mastering how to exploit the financial statements to get the data necessary to make critical decisions. The key is asking two questions— "why?" and "so what?"—and then answering them with data and logic.

Why

Asking why forces the discipline of identifying root causes. In finance, causes are often called *drivers*: revenue drivers, cost drivers, growth drivers. By identifying and managing the drivers, management can use them to push revenues up and costs down, and to accelerate growth.

So What

"So what" questions should be tirelessly asked until it drives you and every-body a little crazy. This includes asking:

- "So what?"
- "So what does this mean?"
- "So what are the action items?"

If you are getting financial data that won't allow any of these questions to be answered, then the question becomes "so what are we doing collecting and looking at this data?" I have seen many long financial (or operational) reports filled with detailed data. But much of that data was never really read or used by anyone. Such data collection becomes a routine and no value is created.

I have included a real-life example of using "why" and "so what" in Appendix A. These two questions are powerful in helping to identify root causes and critical actions. But care must be taken not to alienate people. While some people (maybe your boss) will be impressed by your active and strategic thinking, many others (especially your equals) may react negatively for a variety of reasons:

- It can sound very arrogant if someone else produced the data and you keep asking "why?" or "so what?"
- People may feel intimidated or resentful when asked questions they cannot or are not prepared enough to answer, especially when you are asking them about what they are supposed to be expert in.
- It might cause jealousy. People may perceive you as flaunting your own alleged insight rather than genuinely trying to solve the problem.

If people are alienated, they will not support your brainstorming whole-heartedly. Worse, they may become your political enemies and try to sabotage your effort behind your back. As a result, think carefully about how and when you ask these questions. Some possibilities of making the whys and so-whats less alienating:

- "I am not an expert; Mr. X will know better. Could the reason be . . . ?"
- "I was talking to Mr. X the other day and he mentioned one of the reasons was . . . . What do you think?"
- "If this is the data, could it mean . . . ."
- "I wonder what this means . . . ."
- "I think Mr. X has already implemented some initiatives to deal with this. Maybe the data is indicating we should support him in expanding his effort . . . ."

In short, unless you are with a group of people totally open-minded on brainstorming, it would be advisable to plan and ask the questions in a politically sensitive manner.

An interesting illustration of the need for caution with questions is from the media—I saw the Nicolas Cage movie *National Treasure* a while ago. In the movie, Cage's wife drives him crazy and almost to a divorce because she keeps asking him, "So?" Cage misunderstands her intentions and feels she is constantly pressuring and questioning him. They only manage to reconcile after they rebuild their mutual trust by undergoing a major adventure together and beginning to communicate properly.

IPO: THE HOLY GRAIL?

The initial public offering (IPO) is when shares of a company are first sold to the public and subsequently traded on a public stock exchange. Newspapers are filled with stories about entrepreneurs such as the founders and initial staff of Google, eBay, or Alibaba who became billionaires overnight because of their IPOs. As a result, many aspiring entrepreneurs constantly talk about an IPO as their only end goal. It is worth noting that while IPOs can definitely be good things, they have their downsides. Often, there are other options besides IPO that should not be ignored.

IPOs can be glamorous and lucrative. This is because:

- An IPO is (mostly) for companies that have achieved certain milestones and have an attractive growth potential.
- Capital from an IPO can fund a company's growth.
- Before the IPO, entrepreneurs and other shareholders cannot easily cash out of their investment. The IPO provides liquidity for shares owned by entrepreneurs and pre-IPO investors. This means shares turn from "paper money" to real money.
- An IPO is usually accompanied by significant press coverage and PR effort. Entrepreneurs who started significant companies, like the founders of Google or Amazon, often attract much media coverage and become well-known and prominent public figures.

However, an IPO comes with certain downsides, too:

- IPO itself is a time-consuming and expensive process involving lawyers, bankers, PR agencies, and many others.
- Confidential information such as company strategy and financials have to be disclosed to the public, competitors, and potential competitors.
- Share price and effort to maintain share price may distract management or, worse, lead management to make certain decisions that are focused on the short-term rather than the long-term.
- In countries like the United States, disgruntled shareholders often sue a company and key management when profits are lower than forecast.

An IPO is important because it is one of the most common ways to exit (or "cash out") of a new company. Exit is often necessary for a very practical reason. Many investment funds are not set up to own businesses in perpetuity. They have a defined, finite time horizon and they need to return the invested capital (hopefully, plus a profit) to the fund investors by the end of the agreed period. An IPO is only one way to exit or cash out. Another option is acquisition by another company. While it's less glamorous, acquisition can often be even more attractive than an IPO:

- An IPO requires that a company has reached a certain size. Acquisition does not.
- The acquisition negotiation and due-diligence process, while lengthy, is simpler and less expensive than the IPO process.
- If it is a strategic acquisition, the buyer may be willing to pay a price higher than what would be paid by the public.
- If acquired by a private company or a company of much bigger size, then there is less risk of needing to disclose sensitive information.

Hence, IPO is not the only financial goal for start-ups and smaller companies. In fact, one of the highest profile start-ups in recent HBS history is Eachnet. Its organizers' plan from day one was to copy eBay's model for China. However, since China does not have a developed credit card system and the consumer sophistication found in the West, it was difficult for the company to have an efficient way to charge users and make money. But that was not an issue as the plan was never about making money from consumers. Of course, without a plan to actually make money, an IPO was not even an option. The key target was to sell to eBay. Eachnet's founders bet on the expectation that eBay would find it an invaluable jump-start for the China market and eBay would have so much cash and tradable stocks from its U.S. IPO that it could acquire Eachnet at a very high price. Many investors considered it a very risky strategy and did not invest in Eachnet. But for the few who did, it paid off; they managed to make a significant amount of money when Eachnet was eventually sold to eBay.

Notes

1. Sundem Homgren and Elliot Prentice Hall, *Introduction to Financial Accounting* (Upper Saddle River, N.J.: Prentice Hall, 1998), 494.

2. Robert Knox and James Inkster, "Postdecision Dissonance at Post Time," *Journal of Personality and Social Psychology* 8 (1968): 319–323.
3. Hal Arkes and Catherine Blumer, "The Psychology of Sunk Cost," *Organizational Behavior and Human Decision Process* 35 (1985): 124–140; and Hal Arkes and Laura Hutzel, "The Role of Probability of Success Estimates in the Sunk Cost Effect," *Journal of Behavioural Decision Making* 13(3) (2000): 295–306.
4. John S. Hammond, Ralph L. Keeney, and Howard Raiffa, "The Hidden Traps in Decision Making," in *Harvard Business Review on Decision Making* (Boston: Harvard Business School Press, 2001), 153.

PART III

STRATEGY

11

THE BIG PICTURE

WHAT IS STRATEGY?

Strategy is a sexy word: it is the crown jewel of business concepts, and everyone wants to use it. As the rather trite saying goes, "What good is *doing things right* (efficiency, execution, operations, and so on) if you are not *doing the right things* (strategy)." Strategy conjures up an image of big guys looking at the big picture for the long-term. It is a major compliment at HBS and anywhere in business to be seen or described as a "strategic" thinker.

Strategy is also a promiscuous concept. By this, I mean it has so many different definitions that you can call almost any plan "a strategy." Some examples of the various definitions of the concept of strategy:

- Strategy can be a feature of different organizational levels, such as corporate strategy, business strategy, functional strategy, and so on. Some of these levels have overlapping definitions and add to the confusion; for example, mission can be part of corporate strategy or business strategy.
- Strategy can be about different levels of detail. As author Paul Niven explains, "Some believe strategy is represented by the high-level plans. . . . Others would argue that strategy rests on the specific and detailed actions."[1]

- Strategy can be defined around different types of focus, such as a coherent, unifying, an integrative *pattern* of decisions, an *allocation* of *limited resources*, or an establishment of a *long-term* organizational *purpose*.

These are just a few examples of the wide range of possible definitions of *strategy*. Each definition is important and valuable because it explains a way of looking and thinking about strategy. Much insightful research has been done and hundreds of books have been written on each of the definitions.

While it would be a stimulating intellectual exercise to go through the whole list of definitions, for the purpose of this book, I focus on one simple yet effective choice. Based on HBS learning, my work experience as a strategy consultant, and the messages I have received from readers of my first book, it seems the most appropriate definition for our purpose is to see business strategy (or a *strategy plan*, a term I use interchangeably) as answering two key questions:

- Is this business attractive?
- How do I need to proceed if I mean to win?

To the frustration of a trained engineer like me, answering these two questions is very much an art, not a hard science. It takes judgment, experience, courage, and creativity rather than formulas and checklists. This is because the future is never certain. Strategy is about the future and the future of any market cannot be nailed down. Government policy, economic factors, customer preferences, and competitive landscape are just a few items on an unfathomable list of factors that can never be accurately predicted, even by the most powerful computers and the most experienced strategists.

In addition, the past and present are never perfectly documented. Even if the most powerful computers could be applied to the problem, they would not be able to function effectively without data; as the saying goes: "garbage in, garbage out." However, some element of garbage is unavoidable: the truth involves some confidential information (such as competitive cost structure and competitive market shares); some information that does not exist in any readily available form (such as the impact of economies of scale on cost); some fragments (statistics available for some segments of the market but not others); some that is dated by the time it is published (such as the significant lag time for most government statistics), and so on. Hence, even with computers more powerful than any in existence, you probably would not be able to collect and input enough accurate data to generate the perfect scientific answer.

To make matters worse, situations are seldom if ever identical. So, even the most experienced strategists would not be able to produce an exhaustive checklist of standard, cookie-cutter strategies. No one can give you a menu listing the best way to deal with any business situation, without adaptation.

Luckily for someone like me, strategy is no longer a pure art. In the last few decades, academics, strategy consultants, and business leaders have made much progress in developing tools and best practices that can help bring a significant degree of analytical rigor into strategy and make it into somewhat of a "scientific art" rather than a "pure art." These tools and best practices are very much the focus at HBS:

- Frameworks
- Data management
- Classic strategies
- Process

Frameworks

Frameworks provide effective levers to guide the planning process. Frameworks are structures that delineate the major relevant factors to be considered and the relationship between these factors. Top down–bottom up and supply-and-demand are examples of simple frameworks, as sketched in Figure 11.1. You have two key choices for frameworks:

Figure 11.1 Simple Frameworks

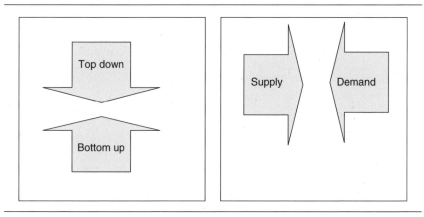

You can adopt a classic framework developed by academics or strategy experts. These frameworks are powerful as they are distilled from years of research and analytical thinking. This is often a good starting point for people new to strategy planning.

In the section below, I discuss the three most well-known and widely used ready-made classic frameworks developed by HBS professors and taught at HBS:

- Porter Five Forces (To answer the question, "Is this an attractive industry?")
- Porter Generic Strategies and Porter Value Chain (To answer the question, "How to achieve sustainable competitive advantages in an industry?")
- Balanced Scorecard (To answer the question, "How to monitor execution?")

Alternatively, you can develop your own framework (I call it DIY—do-it-yourself). As you accumulate more experience in strategy or come to feel that existing frameworks do not fit your needs, you will want to develop your own frameworks. This will usually involve starting from some very basic frameworks (some people call it the skeleton) and then adding details (some people call this fleshing out the skeleton). Top down–bottom up and supply-and-demand are examples of skeletons. Later in this chapter, I present an effective DIY skeleton framework called The Tree. Once a framework is designed, the planning process should systematically analyze each factor of the framework and then synthesize the information into strategic options.

Data Management

Although past and present data will never be perfect, the strategy should still be based on the best data available. Frameworks list only the key factors and issues. Data is needed to analyze the factors and issues. Consultants who make their living doing strategies have developed key best practices and tools for gathering what is available, estimating what is unavailable, checking validity of all the data, and utilizing the data.

Classic Strategies

Even though it is impossible to develop an exhaustive checklist of standard strategies that one can pick and choose to apply to different situations, over the years, some reasonably reliable strategies have emerged. These strategies are useful as references and benchmarks to stimulate brainstorming. They are also useful for defense, as they make good starting points for assessing your competitors' strategy.

Process

An effective planning process can, to a large degree, help manage future uncertainties. The importance of a planning process is succinctly explained by Dwight D. Eisenhower, the 34th president of the United States, when he talked about war:[2]

Plans are nothing; planning is everything.

Because of the uncertainty involved in war (and business), although it may be a bit extreme to say "plans are nothing," there is much truth in President Eisenhower's statement. This does not mean you do not need a strategy. You need a strategy—but must recognize that any strategy can easily and quickly become suboptimal or even ineffective due to the uncertainties involved. As a result, it is critical to know that the process of thinking through and developing the strategy is as important as the plan itself, if not more important. An effective process should be:

- *Systematically exhaustive*. The process should ensure that key factors are prioritized, considered, and analyzed.
- *Explicitly articulated*. The process should also ensure that the factors considered, any assumptions made about them, and the deductive logic behind the strategy are clearly and explicitly articulated and documented. Then when these factors and assumptions change, the strategy can be updated quickly and effectively to address the changes.
- *Execution oriented*. A 1999 *Fortune* magazine research article showed 70 percent of chief executive officer failures were a result of poor execution, not poor strategy. Ever since then, business schools and the business community have realized the importance of not just planning the plan but also planning the execution of the plan.

PORTER FIVE FORCES FRAMEWORK

Is this an attractive industry? This is a million-dollar question for everyone in business—established enterprises need to evaluate their own industry or portfolio of industries as well as possible expansion into other industries; entrepreneurs and investment funds need to assess new markets, and individuals may come across opportunities to invest in private companies.

One of the most well-known and widely adopted frameworks for assessing the attractiveness of an industry is the Porter Five Forces. The framework was conceived by Professor Michael Porter of HBS, one of the world's leading authorities on competitive strategy. This famous framework is taught, discussed, and used not only at HBS but also at many schools and in industry. The simplest version of it is set out in Figure 11.2.

The resultant of the strengths and weaknesses of these five forces will determine if an industry is attractive. At one extreme, if you're looking at a situation where buyers and suppliers have little bargaining power, existing competitors are weak, and the threat from substitutes and new entrants is minimal, then it is most likely a highly attractive industry. The classic example

Figure 11.2   The Five Competitive Forces that Determine Industry Profitability

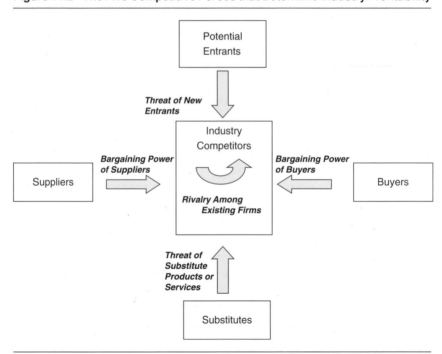

*Source:*Michael E. Porter, *Competitive Advantage—Creating and Sustaining Superior Performance* (New York: Free Press, 1985), 5.

of this is some of the utility monopolies. At the other extreme, if buyers and sellers have strong bargaining power, existing competitors are fierce, and the threat from substitutes and new entrants is significant, then the industry is most likely unattractive. Mom-and-pop stores often fall into this category. Often, the only reason a mom-and-pop store is surviving is that its owners do not draw market-level salary and are satisfied with a low return on capital.

The framework as depicted in Figure 11.2 is simple and elegant. However, to be able to apply the framework effectively, you need to ask how you can tell if suppliers have strong or weak bargaining power. How can you tell if the barrier to entry is high? And so on. To assess the strength of each of the five forces, Professor Porter has developed a comprehensive list of drivers for each of them. By evaluating these drivers, a judgment can be made on the strength of each force. Table 11.1 lists some of the key drivers that I have found most useful in analyzing industry attractiveness.

Of course, some of these drivers, such as industry growth rate, will change over time, so the impact of the change on industry attractiveness must be monitored.

Table 11.1 gives only a partial list. Professor Porter's list is almost exhaustive. It is very useful as a checklist, especially for novices who fear they might forget to consider some key drivers. However, the full list can seem daunting. I was overwhelmed when I first saw it many years ago. But after some practice, you will soon realize that the principle of prioritization, as discussed earlier, definitely applies. As Professor Porter explains, "In a particular industry, not all of the five forces will be equally important and the particular structural factors (or *drivers*) that are important will differ."[3]

High priority should be placed on analyzing the drivers that can affect the business models. Business model can mean "how the business is going to make money," "how the company is going to capture the value it creates," or "who is going to pay for the product or service." Business models include the subscription model, advertising model, commission model, mark-up model, and others. This concept is especially important in businesses involving high technology or new inventions, which have no established or proven business model. Many entrepreneurs at the height of the Internet bubble created value-added businesses that attracted millions of users but failed to find a way to make money from the business (no business model). Some of them were lucky enough to be acquired by bigger businesses that could add them to their core business to make money. But most of them

Table 11.1 Industry Forces and Drivers

Attractive Industry Forces	Possible Key Drivers
High barrier to entry against new entrants	• Existing competitors have proprietary product differences such as patented designs or technology, established brands, and user base. (Example: eBay)
	• Existing competitors have significant cost advantage from experience, supply chain setup, or economy of scale. (Example: Wal-Mart)
	• New entrants would need a large capital to enter the business. (Example: heavy industries)
	• Existing competitors determined to retaliate against aggressive new entrants (Example: the "duopoly" grocery chains in Hong Kong, which have a strong track record of deterring suppliers selling to any new entrant at a competitive price)
	• Buyers will incur high switching cost (training, process, equipment, and so on) or risk that cannot be justified by possible upside from switching. (Example: key machinery in manufacturing)
	• Government regulations discourage new entrants. (Example: commercial banking in China)
Weak supplier power	• Switching cost—risk of moving from one supplier to another or to a substitute product—is low.
	• Buyers have access to numerous relatively small-scale suppliers.
Weak buyer power	• Buyer has limited bargaining power. (Factors: volume by each buyer is relatively small, switching cost or switching risk for buyers is high, and substitute products are limited or nonexistent.
	• Buyer has limited incentive to switch.
Low threat of substitutes	• Buyers will incur high switching cost or risk that cannot be justified by possible upside.
Weak rivalry between existing competitors	• Industry growth is high. (Hence competitors do not have to take market share from each other to grow.)
	• Fixed costs are low and capacity is appropriate. (With constant or intermittent overcapacity, competitors are motivated to slash price to cover fixed costs, as in the airline industry.)
	• Product differences between competitors are high as a result of patented technology or brand identity.
	• Buyers face high switching costs or switching risk.

simply failed when investor money ran out. Often, the critical drivers that need most in-depth analysis become apparent soon after some initial research is done.

PORTER GENERIC STRATEGIES AND PORTER VALUE CHAIN

How do I need to proceed if I mean to win? When it comes to addressing this question, Professor Porter's generic strategy framework is actually frighteningly simple yet most valid. He explains that although there seem to be endless ways a firm can try to compete and many different strengths and weaknesses companies can have versus their competitors, there are fundamentally only two ways to compete successfully—low cost or differentiation, as outlined in Table 11.2.

The two strategies, of low cost and differentiation, can be applied to the broad total market or to a certain segment within the market. The segmented versions are referred to as focus-low-cost or focus-differentiation strategies.

Porter calls low cost, differentiation, and focus (focus-low-cost or focus-differentiation) the three generic strategies. I find the Generic Strategy Framework effective not only as a guide for how to compete, but also as a reminder of how not to compete. If your strategy cannot be categorized into one of the three generic strategies, you risk having no real competitive

Table 11.2 Generic Strategies

Strategy	Selling Price to Buyers	Product or Service	Cost Structure
Low cost	At or near industry average price	Perceived as comparable and acceptable	Lowest cost among competitors
Differentiation	Premium price	Unique along some dimension of value to the buyer	At or near industry average. If cost is higher than industry average, the cost must not be more than the price premium

Figure 11.3 Value Chain Framework

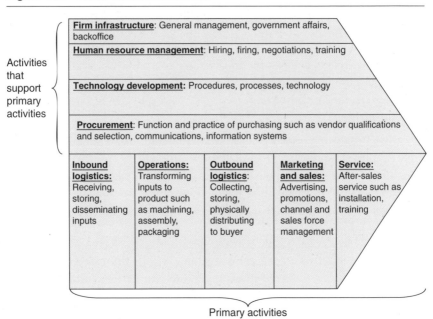

Source: Adapted from Michael E. Porter, *Competitive Advantage—Creating and Sustaining Superior Performance* (New York: Free Press, 1985), 37.

advantage. Your offering is neither lower in cost than your competitors' offering nor differentiated from it. Why should customers buy from you? Unless you have a protected position (such as a monopoly or government license) or you have very weak competitors, you will be unlikely to compete successfully in the industry.

To decide on which generic strategy to adopt and settle on the details (where to save cost and how to differentiate), Porter has developed the value chain framework illustrated in Figure 11.3.

The framework is not rocket science—it is a basic tool to help systematically break down all the key activities a firm performs to be in business. Examining how each of these activities can be done and what impact each has on differentiation and cost makes it possible to see where competitive advantages can come from and which strategy should be adopted to win. For example, say you found out from Porter's Five Forces that a chain supermarket is an attractive business in the city where you live. You then use the value chain to analyze how you could compete if you were to enter. If you find that your strengths would be in efficient procurement, logistics, and operations, then you would probably decide on a low-cost strategy. If you find that your strengths would be in procurement of exotic products and provision of high-end service, you would probably decide on a differentiation strategy. I find the framework a very useful starting point. Primary and supporting activities can be eliminated or added to fit the industry and business for the specific analysis.

WHAT GETS MEASURED GETS DONE: THE BALANCED SCORECARD

As I said in the section on performance measurement for sales, it is simply human nature—*what gets measured gets done*. To ensure execution of strategy, you have to measure progress so it can be monitored and pushed.

Key Performance Indicator, or KPI, has been a hot subject in recent years. The term is self-explanatory—the indicators (or measurements) used to monitor performance. One of the most powerful KPIs used in measuring execution of strategy is the Balanced Scorecard. It is beyond the scope of this book to explain this framework in enough detail for application. When I first tried to implement this framework, I had to read three books and engage a Balanced Scorecard consultant to help me. It seems worth at least describing the concept of the framework, however, as it can stimulate thoughts on how you can design simpler frameworks for your own purposes.

The Balanced Scorecard was developed in the early 1990s by Robert Kaplan, a professor at HBS, and David Norton, a consultant from Boston. Despite its relatively short history, it was hailed by *Harvard Business Review* as one of the 75 most influential ideas of the twentieth century. It is said to have been adopted by at least half of the Fortune 1000 organizations in the United States. Numerous HBS case studies have been written on this subject. In fact, it is seen as such an important concept that Harvard Business Publishing publishes a periodical solely on this subject.[4]

As with the Porter frameworks, the concept of the Balanced Scorecard is not complex. The starting point is to have a vision and a strategy. Vision is where the company wants to be in the long-term. Strategy is what needs to be done to achieve the vision. Figure 11.4 outlines the concept of the Balanced Scorecard.

Figure 11.4 Overview of Balanced Scorecard Framework by Robert S. Kaplan and David P. Norton

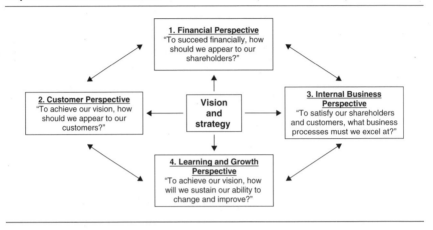

For each of the perspectives, the following scorecard details need to be defined:

- *Objectives* in accordance to strategy and vision
- *Measures* chosen to show whether and to what extent the objective is getting achieved

Figure 11.5 Some Elements from the HBS Mobil Case Balanced Scorecard

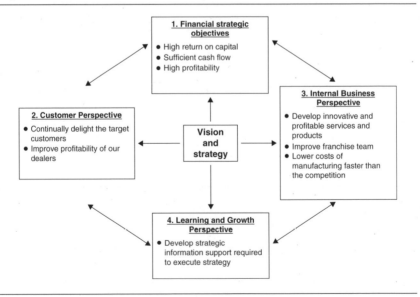

- *Targets* for each measure
- *Initiatives* (or projects) that need to be implemented to achieve the targets and objectives

After the scorecard is defined for all perspectives, regular meetings are held and reports are generated to track actual performance against the targets and to make amendments to the scorecard to fit ever-changing business needs. Incentive systems should be set up to motivate continuous, successful implementation.

Figure 11.5 shows part of the Balanced Scorecard from the HBS Mobil case study, and Table 11.3 sketches the associated scorecard details.[5]

Table 11.3 Customer Perspectives for the HBS Mobil Case (Extract)

Objectives In Accord with Strategy and Vision	Measures Chosen to Track Achievement	Targets for Each Measure for 1995[*]	Initiatives (or Projects) to Achieve the Targets and Objectives
Continually delight the target customers	1. Number of customer complaints	824	None
	2. Mystery shopper rating	82	Develop Mystery Shopper Program where a third-party vendor would purchase gasoline and snacks at each Mobil station on a monthly basis. The shopper would score station's performance on 23 specific items related to service, restrooms, personnel, and other factors.
Improve profitability of our dealers	Total percent gross profit of dealers	60 percent	Develop tool kit for marketing representatives to help dealers in seven business areas, including financial management, convenience stores, and gasoline purchasing.

[*]Numbers disguised to maintain confidentiality.

You may have many questions about the framework—do we need a vision? How to define a vision? Exactly how to look at each perspective? Should we apply a weighting to emphasize the more important indicators? And so on. As discussed, the Balanced Scorecard is not easy to implement. The Mobil exercise took a big team at the company, together with Richard Norton as consultant, eight months just to draft, let alone implement. Therefore, instead of getting into details of the Balanced Scorecard, the key is to recognize the important best practices in driving strategy execution, as highlighted by the Balanced Scorecard framework:

- Measuring strategy execution involves setting clear and explicit objectives, measures, and targets—and then following up on them with a structured process and system that includes regular meetings, regular reporting, and built-in incentives.
- Multiple perspectives are essential. It is tempting to just focus on financial measures, but financial success can be achieved only if customers are satisfied, operations are smooth, and employees are trained and equipped. In addition, financial measures are *lag indicators*—they show the results of actions already taken. To drive strategy, there must also be a focus on *lead indicators*—those measures such as training or equipment that will drive future performance.
- Any indicator is subject to gaming. For example, if only growth is measured, then it is tempting to achieve growth by forgoing profit or other important aspects of the business and strategy. Gaming is reduced by a holistic set of indicators that all work to drive the vision and strategy.
- Communication needs to be explicit. The Balanced Scorecard is not just a measurement tool. It is also a communication tool. It communicates how the vision and the strategy will be achieved. It also communicates that management is serious about execution and following through.

DIY SKELETON FRAMEWORK: THE TREE

One of the easiest skeleton frameworks to use is The Tree. It is widely used not just by management consultants like McKinsey but also in problem solving both within and outside business. The Tree gives a straightforward methodology for you to list out the factors step by step. Four key points about The Tree:

- It starts with a central strategic question. Then it breaks that question down logically one level at a time into subquestions and sub-sub-questions and so on.
- All the questions at the same level should be mutually exclusive so they do not overlap. Overlapping is inefficient as it means duplication. If they overlap, it means the questions can be restructured.
- Taken as a group, the questions and subquestions should be collectively exhaustive. Together, they should cover all the issues that need to be addressed to answer the central question.
- As much as possible, especially at the higher levels, the questions should be closed; that is, they should all have yes-or-no answers. This helps focus on drawing conclusions. As the level gets lower, gradually, closed questions may be replaced by open-ended questions that call for detailed narrative answers.

This process is easier to illustrate with an example. Say the central question is "Can I make money writing a book about HBS?" Figure 11.6 could be part of The Tree.

There is often more than one way of drawing a tree. The way you choose will depend on the issues you want to highlight and the hypothesis you are

Figure 11.6 Part of a Logic Tree

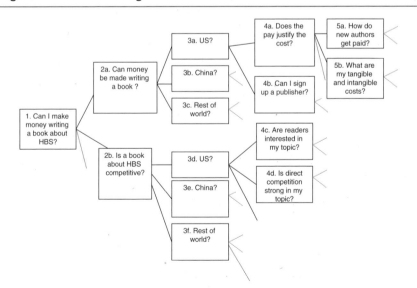

Figure 11.7 Another View of a Logic Tree

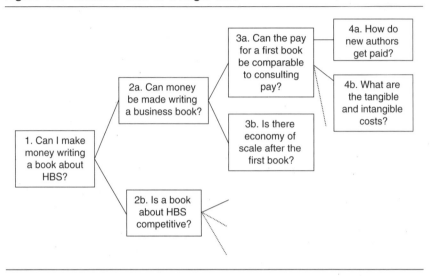

testing. It will also be affected by the way the data is available. If the questions and subquestions are collectively exhaustive, then however you draw The Tree, it should still be able to answer the central question. Figure 11.7 shows another way to draw The Tree for my business book example. The Tree in Figure 11.6 will work better if you believe that the markets in different places are quite different from each other. The one in Figure 11.7 will work better if the you believe that the geographic markets are quite similar and hence need no highlighting.

Notes

1. Paul R. Niven, *Balanced Scorecard Step by Step* (New York: Wiley, 2002), 90.
2. President Eisenhower served as supreme commander of the Allied forces in Europe during the Second World War before he became president. He is well-respected by many for war strategy. Many in the business community found that application of war strategy in business could be very effective.
3. Michael E. Porter, *Competitive Advantage—Creating and Sustaining Superior Performance* (New York: Free Press, 1985), 7.
4. *Balanced Scorecard Report;* subscription available at http://hbp.harvardbusiness.org/ep/subscribe.html.
5. Mobil Corporation's U.S. Marketing and Refining Division. Source: Robert S. Kaplan and Ed Lewis, "Mobile USM&R (A): Linking the Balanced Scorecard," *Harvard Business Review* (May 1997).

12

FILLING IN THE BLANKS

WHAT DATA?

Once you have a framework, the next step is to define the data needed to analyze the factors in the framework and test the hypothesis. The most efficient way to do so is to work backward—first decide on the analysis based on the logic tree (how you are going to use the data) and then collect the data. Using the logic tree for writing a business book presented in Figure 11.6, a worksheet to list out the data needed for one of the questions can look like the one in Figure 12.1.

In this worksheet example:

- The first column is a list of the issues on the logic tree that require analysis to get to an answer. Most issues that need detailed analysis are at the lower levels of the logic tree. As the lower-level issues are analyzed and conclusions drawn, issues at higher levels can be solved based on these outcomes. In this example, by analyzing issues 5a and 5b in Figure 11.6, it may be possible to draw a conclusion on issue 4 without further analysis.
- The second column is the list of analyses planned for each issue. As noted, the most efficient way is to work backward. The worksheet lists the analysis in the format it would be displayed on a PowerPoint slide (or as a diagram in a text document), which might also have a title

Figure 12.1 Assessing Data Needs

Is direct competition strong in my topic (for U.S. market)?

Issue	Analysis	Data source
(1) How strong is existing competition?	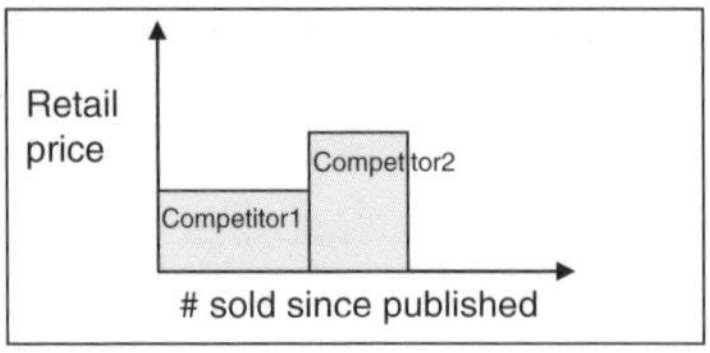 (graph) Retail price / # sold since published, showing Competitor1 and Competitor2	Desk research on best-seller lists and sales data
	Name of book / Author credentials / Strengths of book / Weaknesses of book	Desk research on review by book critics and readers including on Amazon Interviews with key book critics Discussions with focus groups and book clubs
(2) How much new competition is expected in the next 2 years?	Tentative name of book to be published in next 2 years / Author credentials / Content / Key overlap with my book	Desk research including Google, Amazon, publisher Websites Interviews with key publishers and business book critics

drawing a conclusion based on the latest hypothesis. Data needed to complete each analysis is clearly labeled. It should be noted this list of analyses is just a starting point. Most of them will have to be adjusted based on data availability and changes in hypothesis. For example, when I address the first graphical analysis on Figure 12.1, I might discover that it is impossible or will take too much trouble to get data on "# sold since published," but an easily available list shows how many have been sold since year 2000. In this case, I might decide that the analysis can be adjusted to "# sold since 2000" and still be useful for understanding the competition issue. Or, based on interviews, I might find too many competitive books to be displayed in a graph. If so, I might replace this analysis of individual competitive books by another that groups the books into categories for comparison.

• The third column lists sources for the data needed to complete each analysis in the second column.

Both qualitative and quantitative data are important for analysis—and not easy to collect. Of the two, quantitative data is often seen as more valuable.

One of my HBS professors liked to repeat this quote from Lord Kelvin (1883):[1]

> "When you can measure what you are speaking about, and express it in numbers, you know something about it; but when you cannot measure it, when you cannot express it in numbers, your knowledge is of a meager and unsatisfactory kind."

Quantitative data is especially useful because such measures can be synthesized. For example, current market size and growth rate can be multiplied together to estimate future market size. Qualitative comments such as "big market" and "fast growth" cannot be multiplied in the same way.

In addition, quantified measures allow unbiased and unambiguous comparisons of strategic options, scenarios, and trade-offs as well as tangible estimation of resource needs, potential payoffs, and risks. This is a key point as strategy is always about allocation of limited resources—which industry to put your resources (money, time, staff)—and where to invest to develop competitive advantages.

The keys to obtaining effective qualitative and quantitative data are access to a wide range of data sources, ability to deduce unavailable data, discipline to check the data, and pragmatism in using the data.

WHERE FROM?

Starting from the sources easiest to access, these are the key data sources:

- The Internet
- Associations and bureaus
- Interviews
- Analysts' reports
- Professional databases
- Benchmarking
- Sampling

The Internet

Almost everyone knows the Internet is a powerful source of data. For strategy study, you can find the following sources of data online:

- Internet bookshops like Amazon make it very easy to access a wide range of books using search words related to the industries you are studying.

- Websites of key existing and potential players in each of the five forces—suppliers, buyers, competitors, and substitutes—can provide information on your playing field.
- If any existing player is a public company, it will have to file annual reports. These reports will have information on its industries, its performance in each one, its vision and strategy, and its market outlook, as well as its financial data. Often companies will put these reports on their own websites. Most companies will mail you the annual report free if you call up or write to their Investor Relations Department.
- Internet search on Google or Yahoo! with key words including the name of the industry, product, brand names if any, and key companies involved will turn up more information.

Associations and Bureaus

Trade associations, semi-government bodies, and government bureaus collect statistics. Such data is often published and for sale at very reasonable prices. Besides the officially published data, some associations may also be willing, usually for a fee, to provide tailored reports based on both the published data and on the raw data the report was drawn from. This could be useful if the published data do not answer your "logic tree" question but you can see how the raw data behind the report can be analyzed to provide the answer.

Interviews

People with knowledge of the industry—industry veterans, ex-employees, suppliers, buyers, investment bank analysts, and so on—are often willing to talk about what they know. This is one of the fastest and most direct ways to get firsthand information.

When I first started out as a consultant, my job consisted mainly of finding telephone numbers from directories and cold-calling senior executives to set up telephone or face-to-face interviews for my superiors. I was very skeptical when I was first asked to do this. I thought, "Why would people agree to talk to *me*?" but I quickly found out it was easier than I thought. Of course, working for a well-known consulting firm helped as many potential interviewees recognized the name of the firm when I introduced myself over the phone. You would be surprised that many people like talking about themselves and their business, especially if the topic is not confidential or if they see a potential for business in the future. Over the years, I have set up and conducted many interviews. A few best practices I have learned are listed in Appendix B.

Analysts' Reports

Investment banks such as Goldman Sachs hire stock analysts to research and evaluate key industries and key companies in those industries. The analysts then write reports on their findings. One of the purposes of these reports is to enable the bank's private bankers and outside brokers to advise their clients in stock trading. These reports are valuable as analysts often have access to company senior executives who understand that these reports could help stock trading of their companies. Unfortunately, these reports are not freely available. The easiest way to obtain them is via friends or contacts at these banks. This is related to the chapter on social networking. If you do not know anyone, you can try to purchase some of these reports through the Internet either by e-mailing the banks or by searching for some finance Web sites that sell such research reports.

Professional Databases

Professional databases such as Bloomberg and Lexis-Nexis are highly efficient as they give you access to a large selection of journal and newspaper articles using keyword searches. They are available by subscription. Some companies have research departments that subscribe to these services. Otherwise, select libraries, especially business and university libraries, may provide access. Some of these services are also available for individual subscription. You can go onto Google to search for the local sales representatives of these databases. You can contact them to find out about individual subscription or ask for a list of libraries that carry these databases.

Benchmarking

Benchmarking—identifying and studying comparables that can be used as indicators of possibilities or as a comparison to stimulate insights—is a very useful data source. For example, in 2007, a client of mine wanted to evaluate whether to spend R&D dollars on a revolutionary consumer electronics technology. In trying to analyze the Porter Five Forces, we used the Walkman, digital camera, and iPod as benchmarks to understand the product life cycle, speed of copycats, and the like for revolutionary consumer electronics.

In 2000, I was involved in helping a state-owned bank in mainland China determine its strategy in anticipation of the opening up of the financial market to foreign competition. A key component of the study was to analyze the market development and evaluate the successes and failures of state-owned banks in other countries such as Japan that have undergone similar deregulation.

Information on benchmark targets can be found using the kind of sources discussed in connection with other types of data in this section.

Sampling

Sampling involves looking at a relatively few instances to provide an indication of the whole population. Statisticians often talk about "statistical significance," which means you need a certain quantity such as number of surveys before the data collected can be trusted to have an acceptable degree of accuracy. In business, due to time and other resource constraints, it is often difficult if not impossible to get enough data for rigorous significance. But even small samples with no statistical significance could be invaluable as an estimate. For example, a client of mine, a multinational beverage company, once wanted to enter the bottled water business in Thailand. We needed to understand the sales volume of the key competitors, but no data was readily available. So a team of us sat in a rented car across the street from the warehouses of the two biggest competitors and counted the number of truckloads leaving the warehouse every day for one week each. We took pictures of the trucks and found out their capacity from the truck dealers. Based on these daily deliveries, we did some seasonal adjustments and estimated monthly and annual sales volumes.

Another client, an oil refinery in Malaysia, wanted to improve the efficiency of its maintenance process. To understand the workload of the maintenance department, I followed a maintenance technician around for a week and documented all the work he did, how he did it, and how long it took. Then using this as a sample week, I redesigned the process and then calculated the time savings of the new process compared to the week sampled.

THE UNGETTABLES

Very often, critical data do not exist in readily available form and can't be found in a useful amount of time. The ability to deduce these critical numbers is paramount to strategy. These are the techniques taught at HBS that I've found indispensable to any strategist:

- Logical deduction using limited data
- Compound annual growth rate
- Ballpark interview technique
- Scenarios
- Minimum threshold

Logical Deduction Using Limited Data

In most HBS case studies, students get some data either within the text or in table format. But since the cases are based on real-life situations, they reflect the reality that the data available are most often not sufficient to analyze the issues in the case. The key technique needed is to know what you want and then use the numbers given to reach a reasonable estimate. As a simple example, say you need the market size of television sets in city X. In the case study, you are told that the population is 100 million in city X, and that the average life of a television is three years. Assuming no other quantitative data is available from the case write-up, here's one way to estimate the market size:

1. Since city X is in a developed country, assume the average household size is similar to the average U.S. household, around 2.5. This means 100 million people will make 40 million households.
2. Since most families even at the lowest income levels have at least one television, assume each household has 1.5 televisions. Note the total of 40 million × 1.5 or 60 million televisions out there.
3. Assuming their lifespan is three years; about a third of the televisions will need to be replaced every year. This means a market of approximately 40 million × 1.5 televisions × 1/3, or 20 million.
4. Remember that the resulting number, 20 million, is just a ballpark figure and not hard data. Its sensitivity and validity need to be checked using techniques to be discussed in the next sections.

This deductive, logical estimation technique to quantify key parameters based on existing data is a critical tool applicable to many HBS cases and in real-life strategic planning. In fact, this technique is so critical that many consulting firms like to include it as an interview question.

When I was responsible for Greater China recruiting for BCG, for example, my favorite interview question to MBA graduates was "How many

Toyotas do you think there are in Hong Kong?" The interviewees had no access to a computer or even paper and pencil. What I was looking for was the deductive, logical estimation technique, not the exact number. I did not even know the answer myself. I expected something like this: "There are seven million people in Hong Kong. Let's say four people a household. This makes about 1.8 million families. Toyotas are for middle-income families. Let's say about 1/5 of the families are middle income. That makes about 400,000 middle-end cars. Of this market, there are other brands like Honda, Mazda, and Suzuki. None of them seems to have a bigger share than the others. So maybe the number of Toyotas is about 100,000." It does not matter if any of these assumptions are right. The key is the ability to think logically and the comfort with numbers and estimates. Once the logic and comfort are there, researching assumptions and testing their validity is not difficult.

It is useful to reference the two very simple frameworks sketched in Figure 11.1 to help you think of different systematic approaches when undertaking logical deduction:

- *Top down–Bottom up*. Top down means starting from macro numbers and narrowing down until you get to the parameter you are trying to estimate. Bottom up means starting from more granular numbers and expanding until you get to the parameter.
- *Supply-and-Demand*. This is self-explanatory.

The Toyota example is top down, as it starts from macro data population and households and then narrows down. A bottom up approach to the Toyota example will be to start from the number of dealerships, then estimate sales per dealership per month, multiply by 12 months to get an annual figure. Assuming the life of a Toyota is about five years, then multiply by five.

The estimate of Toyotas using demographics is demand-side deduction. Estimate of number of Toyotas based on number of dealerships is supply-side deduction.

Compound Annual Growth Rate

Compound Annual Growth Rate (or CAGR; pronounced KAY-ger) is very useful in logical deduction. CAGR is a critical quantitative concept because it has a very wide range of applications. It was not explicitly taught at HBS—the faculty assumed everyone knew it already!

The concept of CAGR is similar to the idea of compound interest. It is the average annual growth rate when compounding is taken into account. For example, if a market grows from \$1,000 to \$5,000 in five years, the CAGR is 38 percent a year because $\$1,000 \times 1.38 \times 1.38 \times 1.38 \times 1.38 \times 1.38 = \$5,000$. (The growth rate is *not* 500 percent over five years divided by five years.)

The formula is similar to compound interest. The following explains how the formula of CAGR is derived:

$$PV \times (1 + CAGR)n = FV$$

$$\text{Therefore, } (1 + CAGR)^n = FV/PV$$

$$1 + CAGR = (FV/PV)^{(1/n)}$$

$$CAGR = (FV/PV)^{(1/n)} - 1$$

where FV is the future or ending value, PV is the present or starting value, and *n* is the number of years between PV and FV. This formula is best explained by examples:

Example one: If the widget market was worth \$300 million in 2000 and in 2007 it is \$400 million, then $n = 2007 - 2000 = 7$. CAGR is $(400/300)^{(1/7)} - 1 = 4\%$

Example two: If the historical average CAGR for the market in the last three years is 15 percent per year, the forecast market size in five years if it continues to grow at the same rate would be

Future market size = Current market size $\times (1 + 15 \text{ percent})^5$

Example three: Sales of company X doubled in the last four years. Doubled means $(FV/PV) = 2$. Hence

$CAGR = 2^{(1/4)} - 1 = $ roughly 20 percent

CAGR is extremely useful in the estimation of key parameters. For example:

- Historical CAGR can be used as the basis for estimating the future, as illustrated in example two. Often historical CAGR is adjusted up or down based on qualitative data. For example, if the market in example two is expected to slow down in growth in the next few years, then historical CAGR of 15 percent can be seen as the maximum growth rate and 10 percent or 12 percent could be used in the formula rather than 15 percent (picking the number involves an assessment of sensitivity, multiple estimates, and triangulation that will help ensure that the 10 percent or 12 percent used is valid even though it is a rough estimate. These techniques will be discussed later in the chapter.) In addition to market size, CAGR can be applied to competitors' size and growth, price growth, and other growth estimates.

- Often, your data from interviews or trade journals will not give a growth rate. An interviewee may say "doubled in five years" or the trade journal may read "expected to treble in the next 10 years." CAGR will allow you to work out a growth rate that can be used either to estimate the future market or business size or for comparison with other industries.
- Once you have CAGR, it is easy to assess this growth rate by comparing to benchmarks like GDP growth, inflation, or stock index growth to judge if the growth rate is attractive.

To look smart, many MBA graduates use a shortcut calculation of CAGR. I call it the Rule of 75%. It goes like this:

CAGR roughly equals 0.75 divided by the number of years the factor in question takes to double.

Using this rule on example three, CAGR roughly equals

$$0.75/4 = 0.19 \text{ (or roughly 20 percent)}$$

Appendix C shows the accuracy of this rule. This rule is useful to quickly work out CAGR in your head (or if you are trying to show off your skills in a discussion).

Ballpark Interview Technique

When you try to do your research through interviewing, you will notice that many interviewees are reluctant to give quantified data. This greatly affects the value of the interviews. Without quantification, you really do not know what people mean when they give qualitative data like "fast" or "slow," "big" or "small." Usually it is not because they do not want to quantify but because they do not have the data and feel they don't wish to be held responsible for giving the wrong number. What they do not understand is even a rough estimate is very useful as a start for quantification for strategy planning. "Ballpark technique," as I call it, often works to help to get at least a rough estimate from interviewees. It involves giving the interviewee a few options to choose from. These options are sufficiently different from each other that they make the choice relatively easy. Once a "ballpark" option is chosen, further narrowing down can be done until the interviewee cannot provide further information. To demonstrate the technique, here is a possible conversation between an interviewer and an interviewee:

> INTERVIEWER TRYING TO GET DATA: How fast do you think the refrigerator market has been growing in the last few years?
>
> INTERVIEWEE: I don't know. I don't have any data.
>
> INTERVIEWER: Well, do you think it is closer to 0.5 percent, five percent, 15 percent, or over 25 percent?
>
> INTERVIEWEE: It has been slow but not completely no growth, probably closer to five percent than 15 percent.
>
> INTERVIEWER: Do you think it is more like three to six percent or more like six to nine percent.
>
> INTERVIEWEE: Don't know but probably lower than higher.
>
> INTERVIEWER: So it is roughly three to six percent from your estimate?
>
> INTERVIEWEE: Maybe.

Like the results of logical deduction, these ballpark figures need to be checked and rechecked. But at least this approach gives you a starting point for the necessary estimates.

Scenarios

If a key parameter is very difficult (or impossible) to estimate but yet very important to your strategy plan, a tool you can use is *scenarios*—asking "what if?" The idea is to define a few scenarios for your target parameter and then compare and evaluate the implications of the outcomes from various scenarios. Using the television example, say the market growth rate is very difficult to estimate. You have looked at all research reports and interviewed many people but you are not getting any reasonable ballpark estimates. So you decide to define three scenarios and then investigate the implications of each:

Scenarios on Market CAGR from Now Until 2015
Pessimistic: zero growth
Average performance: five percent per year
Optimistic: 10 percent per year

A few points illustrated by this example:

- There are only three scenarios. It is important to limit the number of scenarios, as trying to set up too many will create confusion and distraction.
- This example is about estimating one parameter. It is advisable to apply scenarios to not more than a handful of parameters. Applying scenarios to too many parameters will also create confusion and distraction.
- Scenarios should be defined based on careful consideration of all information available. They should be realistic.
- It is useful to choose scenarios that will demonstrate the range of outcomes like the one shown here. Other choices include maximum, average, minimum; aggressive, base case, passive; or base case, accelerated, explosive. Base case can be the middle-of-the-road scenario (the "basic" scenario) or the most likely scenario depending on the analysis.

Minimum Threshold

If scenario analysis still makes it too difficult to estimate a parameter due to the huge range of possibilities, defining the minimum threshold could be a possible tool. Say you find that x percent per year market growth is the minimum needed to make an investment attractive. Then the question is whether you believe this market growth is possible.

CONSISTENCY AND TRIANGULATION

Naturally, the accuracy and validity of data estimated by deduction and data from sources such as interviews must be checked. Even data obtained from seemingly reliable sources should be checked. A few years ago, I used some population data straight from a China provincial government statistics book. The table I set up looked something like the one shown in Table 12.1 (though the reported data have been disguised, they follow the same pattern as the original).

I was rushing to do my analysis so I did not spend time to think about the data. I just copied the data. In the middle of my presentation, my client pointed out that the population of the cities and non-city areas within the province added up to more than the total for the province! Needless to say, the mistake affected the credibility of the whole presentation.

Table 12.1 Population Estimates

Place	Population 2003 (Millions)
City 1 in this province	10.2
City 2 in this province	4.4
City 3 in this province	3.3
Non-city areas within this province	30.4
Total for this province	45.4

Therefore, it cannot be overemphasized: check your data whenever possible. Two of the most direct ways for ensuring data accuracy are checking it for consistency and triangulating the item in question.

Consistency

If a certain parameter is important to the strategy, then multiple sources of data or deduction tools should be used. The results should be compared against each other. Since data from interviews and data deduced by tools are often rough ballpark figures, you can't expect the figures to be identical, even if they are all consistent and valid. It's only necessary for them to be "within each other's range." For example, if CAGR resulted in an estimate of market size of $2 billion and the top-down tool resulted in $1.8 billion, then these rough estimates can possibly be considered consistent. However, if you got $2 billion in the former and $1 billion in the latter, then you should revisit your estimates. There is no fixed definition of what "within range" is. It depends on the accuracy you need for your analysis. In most cases, a 10 to 15 percent difference could be acceptable for rough estimates. A difference of 30 percent or more is not so acceptable. When two or more estimates are "within range" but not exactly the same, a usual practice is either to take the average or use a range with a minimum and a maximum.

Triangulation

Data for different parameters must *triangulate:* They must make sense when they are put together. In the population data example shown in Table 12.1, the data for individual cities and the total for the province do not

Table 12.2 Reported Percentage within Each Key Market

	United States (%)	Canada (%)	Australia (%)	China (%)
Top end	39	26	23	37
Middle	41	43	29	39
Low end	20	31	58	24

triangulate—they do not make sense when put together. Another example: suppose you are estimating market shares of major competitors. In that case, the sum of the percentage shares of major competitors should not exceed 100. If you have sales estimates for various competitors, the total should not exceed the estimated total market. If you have historical 2006 market sales and estimates for 2007 sales, 2007 sales should be reasonably larger than 2006 if it is a growing market. And so on.

Besides being very effective for testing validity when you attempt different ways to estimate a key parameter, triangulation is also extremely useful when you have to assess other people's estimates quickly. It is surprising that even professional consultants often publish reports or give presentations that contain data that do not triangulate. Table 12.2 shows an example I recently saw in a professional presentation by a real estate consultant from Canada.

Do you see the problem in the table? The Australia market adds up to 110 percent! Sometimes this kind of discrepancy is a typographical error, but sometimes it is a real estimation problem. Once you have the concept of triangulation ingrained in you, you will be able to pick these mistakes out quickly. You may be able to help a company avoid a wrong decision based on a mistake in a critical parameter. Even if the error is not in a critical parameter, you can look smart and alert in front of your superiors or clients (this is one of the key skills that often make MBAs look smarter than they are). But you must be careful not to point out the mistake in a way that will embarrass the creator of the estimate. This is related to social networking—it is always better to make friends rather than enemies.

The more important the data, the more checking needs to be done. One of the key measures of importance is sensitivity. *Sensitivity* here means how much the data affect the decision you are trying to make. For example, if you are looking at a business with high fixed costs, then revenue projections are very important since once fixed cost is covered, every dollar of revenue largely goes to the net profit with very little lost due to variable cost.

LAW OF ACCURACY

Estimates often require further calculation: you need to add, multiply, subtract, or divide them to get the results you're after. For example, if you estimate a market to be around $25 million and market share of a certain company is about one third, using the calculator gets you something like this:

$$\$25,000,000 \times 1/3 = \$8,333,333.33$$

Some people are tempted to report this kind of number as the estimated company sales. But publishing it as it stands would violate a very important mathematical rule: the "Law of Accuracy" (see below).

The "Law of Accuracy"

When combining estimates with different numbers of significant figures, the accuracy of the result can be no greater than the least accurate of the estimates. This means when estimates are added, subtracted, multiplied, or divided, the result should not have more significant figures than the original estimates.

The number of significant figures is *the number of digits that have some degree of accuracy, plus the last digit.* Most MBAs are not mathematicians and tend not get too technical or exact in the definition of significant figures (details such as when zero is counted as a significant figure and when it is not; which digits have some degree of accuracy and which do not; and what it really means to say "plus the last digit," and so on).

The important point is to recognize that often an estimate could be derived so roughly that it has only one or two significant figures. For example, an eight-digit derived estimate like $25 million is apt to mean only that the number is somewhere between $20 million and $30 million. As a result, combinations of estimated data must not include excessive numbers of significant figures or decimal places. For example, when you encounter a number such as the $8,333,333 that came up in the calculation based on the $25 million market estimate, the appropriate interpretation is often "somewhere between $8 million and $9 million, but probably on the low side," so it can be rounded to $8 million or $8.5 million. If further combinations (addition, multiplication, and so on), especially on a spreadsheet, are necessary, then, for simplicity, most people would choose to continue to carry the $8,333,333. This is OK as long as the final number presented is rounded appropriately. For example, you might want to know what the total would look like if the sales of $8,333,333 grew 40 percent. You could calculate $8,333,333 \times 1.4$ (that is, 140 percent) on your spreadsheet or calculator ($11,666,666) and then round the output to $12 million or a range for use in presentations and decision making.

KEEP YOUR SENSE OF PERSPECTIVE

As you use these detailed tools for estimating and checking data to try to get the data for strategy, it is critical to keep your perspective on what this all means.

So What?

I was watching television one night, and this conversation between a grown man and an eight-year-old girl really amused me:

> MAN (A FRIEND OF THE CHILD'S FATHER): Hello, Daisy. It's nice to meet you. You look just like your mom.
> CHILD: So what?
> MAN: Oh . . . I mean you are as pretty as your mom.
> CHILD: So what?

I believe this child will do well in data analysis.

"So what?" is the paramount question in data analysis. Data is a means, not an end. The key skill is to be able to ask "so what" constantly, from the time you are planning your data collection to the time you are applying the data. You found out the biggest competitor has a 50 percent market share. So what? What does it mean to your hypothesis? Would your strategy be different if the share was 40 percent or 60 percent? Do you need to verify this data or is this ballpark estimate good enough? In fact, at BCG, we are not allowed to write any PowerPoint presentation slides or draw any graphs without a "so what" as the title or at the bottom of the slide. The idea behind this rule is to force the thinking on "so what" for every single analysis.

An example from my consulting work:

A client of mine, a multinational beverage company, wanted to enter the bottled water business in Thailand. If the market turned out to be attractive, then the two options for entry were "greenfield" (start building from scratch) or "acquire a small brand and grow it." The first phase of the project was to study the Porter Five Forces to confirm marketing attractiveness. The second phase was to compare the cost of the two options. One late night during the second phase, I finally finished assessing the cost of the greenfield option and the cost of acquiring the small brand (not including growing the brand). I was about to start evaluating the cost of growing the small brand when I realized that the estimated acquisition cost for the small brand was already more than triple the cost of greenfield. The difference was sufficiently big to force the conclusion that greenfield would be the cheaper option. Then it dawned on me that it was irrelevant to estimate the cost of growing the small brand because it would not change the conclusion. This realization saved the team and me a lot of time and effort.

It is not always easy to tell "so what" right after you have collected (and verified) the data. For many kinds of data, benchmarking comparables could be a useful tool. For example, suppose you found out a company in the IT industry in Malaysia has a growth rate of 15 percent per year. Is this a strong or weak growth rate? In such cases, it is useful to compare this to benchmarks, such as growth of the IT industry in Malaysia, competitors in Malaysia and overseas, the company's own history, or other companies in your portfolio.

Sometimes, absolute numbers need to be converted into ratios for comparison. For example, a reader once asked me: "I want to invest in this company B. It has a debt of US$50 million. Is that high or low?" It is difficult to tell whether this is high or low because it depends on factors including the company's current and future ability to repay the debt. To assess the level, the debt can be converted into ratios such as debt/equity or "times interest earned."[2] Then the ratios can be compared to benchmarks such as industry average, competitors' ratios, the company's own history, bank requirements, or rating agency requirements.[3]

As another example, suppose you see that a company has $100 million net profit. To assess if this is sizable, you can compare it with the net profits of competitors or other companies of interest to you. You can also calculate market share or net margin (net profit divided by revenues) to assess the company's market importance and its ability to turn each dollar of revenue into net profit.

Decisions on what ratio to quantify and benchmark for each strategic study will depend on the hypothesis and framework you have selected.

Stop Fooling Yourself

As a trained engineer, I used to think a good strategist should be able to give a definite answer with confidence: "This is what the data says and this is what we should do." No one told me otherwise until I overheard a senior consulting partner saying, "Vic (a starting consultant like me) is great. He knows to use the word *seem* and the phrase *the data seem to show that* even on day one. He has the right perspective on data. I can't say the same about Emily." A light bulb went on in my head. I realized that instead of pretending that the data is perfect and will give a definite answer, I should acknowledge that the data is imperfect and is most often only ballpark and directional. Using "seem" and "seem to indicate," both in thought and in discussion, provides a constant reminder of reality and also stimulates more brainstorming, inviting constructive challenges from others that can increase the validity of the strategy.

Don't Work Your Data Too Hard

If you massage the data enough, they will say what you want. This third point is very much related to the two that precede it. As discussed, you have to use data to deduce "so what." But the data is imperfect—it includes all kinds of estimates. This will mean that very often, data can be deliberately manipulated to drive a certain direction or decision. Think of an eight-ounce glass containing four ounces of water: it can be described as "half full" or "half empty," which can lead to very different "so what" conclusions. Or say the glass is 75 percent full of water. It can be rounded down to 50 percent full or rounded up to 100 percent full, which again can lead to very different answers to "so what." Hence, it is important when you are analyzing data or when you are presented with analysis to keep this maxim in mind: "If you massage your data enough, they will say anything you want."

Notes

1. Lord Kelvin (William Thompson) was an Irish mathematical physicist and engineer widely known for developing the Kelvin scale of absolute temperature measurement.
2. These are just examples of ratios used in accounting and finance. Debt/equity = total liabilities of the company divided by total shareholders equity. It measures what part of a company's resources is obtained from borrowing and what part is from owners' investments. The calculation of times interest earned = (pretax income + interest expense)/interest expense. It measures a company's ability to make the interest payment.
3. Rating agencies such as Standard & Poor's Corporation or Moody's rate bonds issued by companies on their creditworthiness, such as AAA, AA, A . . . B and so on. Their ratings are guided by lists of objective requirements including the range or thresholds for various debt ratios.

13

"PLANS ARE NOTHING.

PLANNING IS EVERYTHING"

One way to look at the overall planning process is that of a quest for "the story." Frameworks list factors. Data help assess and analyze each of these factors. Outcomes of assessment and analysis organized logically tell the story of each factor. The overall planning goal is to organize the stories of the key factors into one overall story.

For the "how" of constructing of a story, see "'A' for Articulate" in Chapter 3. This chapter takes up the "when" of constructing the story and then the fitting together of "how" and "when" in the discipline "elevator pitch." Finally, it illustrates this concept with an example.

When to Construct the Story

If possible, start a story as soon as you have some initial data. The story at that point is fiction based on limited data. Officially, this fiction is called "hypothesis." The framework and data collection are then designed to focus on proving or disproving the hypothesis. As you collect data,

195

Figure 13.1 Hypothesis to Strategy

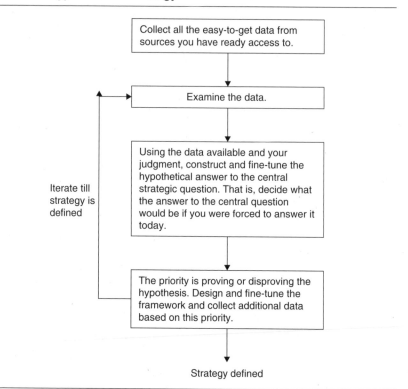

update the hypothesis and adjust the framework and data collection plan accordingly.

The iterative process is depicted in Figure 13.1.

When I learned this technique during my first days as a strategy consultant, I did not believe in it. It bothered me that the initial hypothesis is often generated very quickly after only very superficial data research, and that once an initial hypothesis is generated, the framework and data collection are very much biased toward proving it. I felt it was just a way for strategy consultants to get to an answer (not necessarily "the right" answer) quickly. But I soon noticed the benefits of using a hypothesis:

- More often than not, the hypothesis based on limited data is directionally correct—it won't be precisely true, but it is apt to point toward the final answer. This could be another manifestation of the 80/20 rule I discussed earlier.

- Even when the hypothesis is not correct, the process is iterative, so hypotheses, frameworks, and data collection are all quickly adjusted.
- The resulting focus is effective in facilitating and prioritizing the data collection process.

Elevator Pitch

The best strategists are experts at the "elevator pitch." That is, imagine you found yourself unexpectedly sharing an elevator with the big boss or a potential investor; you should be able to tell the summarized version of the story during the ride. You should be finished by the time the elevator doors open again. The big boss or potential investor should be able to understand the logic and conclusion. The elevator pitch helps drive story-telling, because with such limited time, the logic must be tight and convincing. It also drives hypothesis iteration from the start. Since you are expected to have an "elevator pitch" ready at any time, you must have a hypothesis on hand at any time.

To illustrate the concept of storytelling and hypothesis, I return to my strategic question, "Can I make money writing a book about HBS?" Say after some initial discussions with author friends and some Internet research, I find good market potential for a business book like this one. The easiest market to enter is China with its state-owned presses. The most difficult one is the United States, since it is a very sophisticated market. However, John Wiley and Sons, a major U.S. publisher, has a Singapore office, which may make it easier to reach that market. Authors are paid a percentage of the sales. The percentage is quite standard for new authors, but it is enough to be lucrative as I can write the book when I have time. It will not interfere with my other work or personal life. Hence the opportunity cost of writing the book is insignificant.

Based on this line of reasoning, my hypothesis to answer the strategic question looks like this:

I can make money writing a book on HBS if:
- I first enter the Chinese market with a Chinese version, followed by entering the U.S. market with an English version.
- I sign up a state-owned press for the Chinese market and then market the book to John Wiley & Sons.
- I get the standard new author deal with a time line that allows me to write at my own pace.

Overall, this is inductive logic, as all the bullet points are parallel and all support the conclusion. Then each point can be broken down further for details. For example, the second bullet point can be broken down to further details:

- I sign up a state-owned press for the Chinese market and then market the book to John Wiley and Sons.
  - Getting published by a Chinese state-owned press can build my book's credibility.
  - Credibility is one of the selection criteria at John Wiley and Sons.
  - Therefore, getting published by a Chinese state-owned press can help me approach John Wiley and Sons.

This is an example of deductive logic. The tree and the data collection will be designed to put more (not all) focus on proving and disapproving all the logical arguments leading to the answer of the central strategic question. Figure 13.2 shows an example of part of the resulting logic tree, with the hypothesis marked in bold italics:

Figure 13.2 Annotated Logic Tree

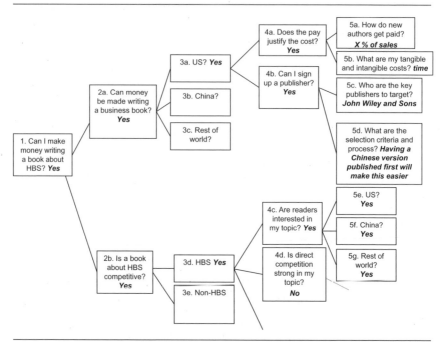

The branches of the tree should be further developed until all key details are covered. As more data is collected, the hypothesis, the framework, and data collection focus will be adjusted. A well-designed framework is collectively exhaustive. Therefore, even if the hypothesis turns out to be wrong, the framework is often still valid. It is only the focus of research that needs to be reorganized. The iteration of data gathering and fine-tuning continues until a satisfactory answer for the central strategic question is obtained.

TIME LINE

Storytelling is the tool to manage the content of the planning process. I find the "time line" a useful tool to manage the progress of the process itself. Figure 13.3 is an example of a time line format consultants often use:

These are the key components of the time line:

- The timing of the project. Most strategy studies take three to six months.
- The key work modules and the timing for each. Two points to note:

Figure 13.3 Process Time Line

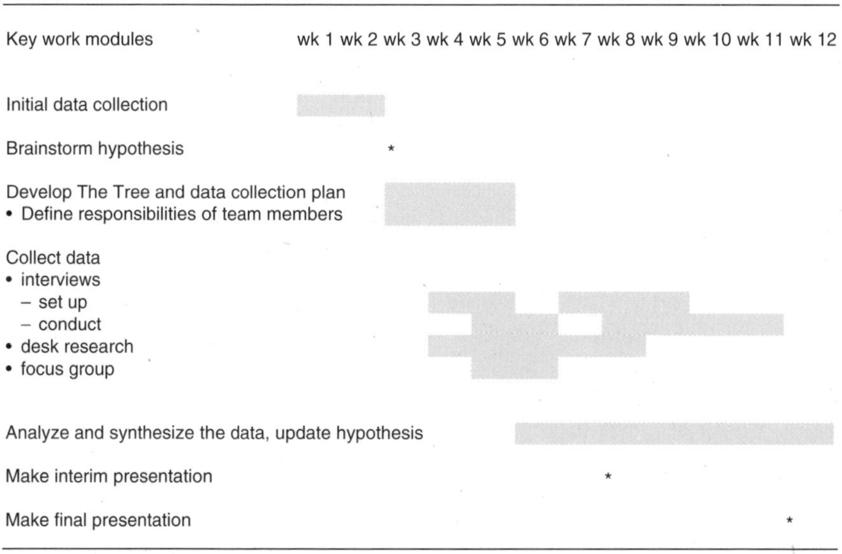

Key work modules	wk 1	wk 2	wk 3	wk 4	wk 5	wk 6	wk 7	wk 8	wk 9	wk 10	wk 11	wk 12
Initial data collection		▓										
Brainstorm hypothesis			*									
Develop The Tree and data collection plan • Define responsibilities of team members			▓	▓								
Collect data • interviews – set up – conduct • desk research • focus group					▓	▓	▓	▓				
Analyze and synthesize the data, update hypothesis						▓	▓	▓	▓	▓	▓	
Make interim presentation							*					
Make final presentation												*

- As explained before, data collection and hypothesis enhancement should be an iterative process rather than a sequential process. This can be seen by the overlapping timing of these work modules.
- Work almost always takes much longer than seems likely initially. Unexpected delays and unavoidable inefficiencies almost always happen. As discussed in an earlier chapter, I have a "1.5x rule." If a planning module looks like it will take 1 month, I will put 1.5 months in the plan. If it looks like it will take 2 months, I will plan for 3 months. This is not to build buffer or slack. My experience shows that 1.5x is just barely enough time.
- This process does not include developing Key Performance Indicators for monitoring strategy execution. This is because there is usually a time lag between a report on strategy recommendation and implementation. The strategy report will need buy-in and approval from the board and top management. Then the plan may have to be fine-tuned before implementation planning can start. Hence the KPI for monitoring strategy execution is usually a separate follow-on effort with its own time line rather than lumped together with strategy study.
- Specialized software can be used for detailed time line planning. This kind of program can be very useful for details, but I have found Microsoft Excel sufficient for high-level planning.
- Interim and final reporting are formal communications to the stakeholders. They are key milestones within the time line. Such reporting is important to update the stakeholders on progress, get their feedback, and force the team to put the data and story on paper to help focus the rest of the work. But care must be taken, because interim reports are time-consuming to prepare. The number and timing of interim presentations should balance the cost and the benefit.

THE BIG PICTURE

Frameworks, data, logic, and time lines are about getting to the details. Details are critical for an effective strategy and strategy planning process. However, it is easy to get so engrossed by the details that one loses sight of the big picture. Here are a few best practices related to strategy that I have found invaluable whenever I feel overwhelmed by details:

Warren Buffett's "smart people dumb people" reality check. A friend of mine at business school told me a piece of advice he said he has heard directly from Warren Buffett. It goes something like this: *Find an industry where average people can make a lot of money, not an industry where even smart people struggle to make a little money.* This is indeed a major insight and a valuable sniff test. It absolutely does not replace analysis and all the details—Buffett himself has a team conducting industry analysis. But it does provide a valuable big picture reality check.

Professor Bill Sahlman's people test. Sahlman is one of the star professors at HBS. He taught me entrepreneurial finance there. One of the cases discussed in the class was Business Research Corp. In the case, Business Research Corp needed more capital to finance a new business opportunity entailing electronic delivery of Wall Street research to institutional investors. After the two-hour session, the class voted on whether to invest in this new opportunity. Most people in the class voted no. Professor Sahlman then said, "I might have voted no also based on all these analyses. But there is one critical point missing: the person doing this was Jeffrey Parker. Parker is not only a successful serial entrepreneur but also someone who knows the market very well. In entrepreneurial ventures when many things are uncertain, the entrepreneur makes a critical difference."

It is the future that counts. When analyzing and considering the frameworks and data, an invaluable discipline is to look at the future, not only the present. It is important to dream up possible changes you can bring to benefit your goal, as well as possible changes that will affect the industry and your position. You should consider the offensive and defensive moves necessary to meet and, better still, exploit these changes. Steve Jobs, the man who founded and rescued Apple Computer, is the master of exploitation of change. In 1998, when asked how he could make Apple a major player given the dominance of Wintel, he answered: "I will wait for the next big change."[1] He later founded Pixar and then iPod, both times exploiting the major changes in technology.

Note

1. Dan P. Lovallo and Lenny T. Mendonca, "Strategy's Strategist: An Interview with Richard Rumelt," *McKinsey Quarterly* no. 4 (November 2007).

14

THE CLASSICS

Razor and Blade

At HBS, some classic strategies are always being discussed[1]. These strategies have achieved some high-profile success in the past and can potentially be applied to or used as benchmarks for new business situations. In addition to the benefits of adopting or adapting these strategies for your own work, they are also very useful aids to the analysis of other companies' strategy or to conversation with seasoned businesspeople.

The first of these goes by the name of the "razor and blade" strategy. It is also often referred to as "bait and hook" strategy. The strategy is to sell an initial master product at a low price and then make money on highly profitable consumables that must be purchased over and over to keep using the master product.

This strategy originated from the razor company Gillette. Gillette used this strategy, selling razor handles at a very competitive price and then making money from the disposable blades that had to be replaced as the razor was used. This strategy continues to be used in the disposable razor blade market to this day.

When I was at BCG, we used this strategy to help a major telecom equipment manufacturer turn from losing money to making a profit. The client sold major telephone switches to telephone carriers. Its profits were depressed and it was under tremendous government and market pressure not to increase price on the switches.

When we studied product profitability, we found that the company could significantly increase its profit by increasing prices on cables. This worked because, although the unit cost of the cables was low, their sales volume was big. While a telephone company might only buy a few new switches each year, it had to buy new cables for not only the new switches but all the old switches it had. In addition, cables were not a major focus for the regulators or for customers who were focusing on capital cost at that time. Replacing cables for old units was considered a maintenance expense. Since telephone companies had a wide range of equipment to maintain besides the switches, the cost of cables was only a small portion of their annual maintenance cost.

The project recommended that the client gradually increase the price of the cables. The client became profitable within one year after.

Loss Leader

A *loss leader* is an item sold below cost in order to stimulate other sales at a profit. Supermarkets often use this technique, advertising a few items at prices below cost to attract customers and create the image of low price. The supermarket expects that the typical customer will purchase other items at the same time, either for convenience or because of the image of "low price" created by the loss leader, and the profit on these other items will more than make up from the loss on sales of the loss leader.

Southwest Airlines

The idea behind this strategy (based on the success and profitability of Southwest Airlines) is that when a low-cost, aggressive, and innovative company enters the market, the company not only succeeds, it also dramatically changes the overall market, leading to tremendous growth for both the company and the market.

Southwest Airlines was incorporated in the United States only about 40 years ago. Its first flight was in 1971. Its mission is to make flying less expensive than driving between two points. Key components of its low-cost strategy include lean operations, such as no in-flight meals and no business class or first class seating, along with high productivity, such as rapid turn-around to minimize time aircraft spend on the ground. Combined with competitive customer service and effective marketing, these decisions made Southwest one of the world's most profitable airlines and also drove explosive growth of the market due to the low fares on offer. Southwest Airlines not only took market share from other airlines, it grew the total market (or the "whole pie," as MBAs like to call it) since fares became low enough to compete with other modes of transportation like driving or riding the bus and also low enough to encourage increased travel. Nowadays, the Southwest Airlines model is applied not only as a strategy for airlines worldwide but also as a possible strategy for other industries including retailing and banking.

MERGERS AND ACQUISITIONS

In business, a merger is usually the combination of two companies but can involve more companies joining into a larger one. An acquisition, or takeover, is the purchase of one company by another.

Mergers and acquisitions (commonly referred to as M&A) is a well-known business strategy. The key reasons usually given for an M&A are to grow revenues, reduce cost, or both. This is the famous $1 + 1 = 3$ synergy argument. Examples of M&A targeting growth include Microsoft acquiring start-ups for access to their new technologies and talent; HSBC acquiring banks worldwide to generate revenue growth; and Sony acquiring Columbia Pictures to control the software in order to drive its hardware sales. Examples of M&A targeting cost savings through consolidation, scale, or efficiency include the merger of Universal Music and Polygram Music, where offices in each country were merged, or a profitable company acquiring a company with accumulated tax losses so the tax losses can shelter the positive earnings of the acquirer and hence reduce taxes.

However, while it is well-known, M&A is a strategy difficult to execute well. A number of studies have shown that $1 + 1$ can often become less than 2 instead of more:

- In *A Note on Mergers and Acquisitions and Valuation*, published by Richard Ivey School of Business, some McKinsey & Company studies were quoted. The studies found that M&A efforts were not always successful for either acquired companies or acquirers:
  - Prior to being acquired, 24 percent of the companies studied were performing better than their industry average and 53 percent were among the top quartile of their industry. After the acquisition, these figures dropped to 10 percent and 15 percent respectively.[2]

- Fully 60 percent acquirers failed to make a positive return on the cost of the capital they invested in the acquisitions.[3]
- Another slightly dated but widely quoted study was published by Michael C. Jensen and Richard S. Ruback of HBS in 1983. They studied the results of mergers over a period of 11 years, and found that in mergers, the average return to shareholders of the acquiring company was 0 percent. The return was four percent in acquisitions involving a public offer to the shareholders of the target company.[4]
- Warren Buffett described his views of acquisitions in his 1981 Berkshire Hathaway Annual Report in a rather humorous analogy:

  "Many managers were apparently over-exposed in impressionable childhood years to the story in which the imprisoned, handsome prince is released from the toad's body by a kiss from the beautiful princess. Consequently they are certain that the managerial kiss will do wonders for the profitability of the target company (the prospective acquisition). . . . We've observed many kisses, but very few miracles. Nevertheless, many managerial princesses remain serenely confident about the future potency of their kisses, even after their corporate backyards are knee-deep in unresponsive toads."

One of the key reasons of failure is the difficulty in executing post-merger integration (or PMI) to realize all the planned synergies. Examples of such difficulties include departure of key staff members due to power struggles, culture clashes, or other personnel reasons, technical difficulties such as incompatible information systems, ineffective PMI execution due to time or other pressures, or simply misrepresentation by certain parties before the merger. I was charged with doing due diligence for a major multinational home appliance brand considering acquiring a leading brand in China. The target company organized a due diligence trip for me to visit their headquarters in Guangzhou, China. After I studied all the paperwork in their office, they took me to the biggest local department store. I saw long lines of consumers queuing to buy their appliances. I was impressed, as I have never seen such queues for major appliances anywhere in the world. But I also got suspicious and later discovered through talking to a junior salesman at the department store that those consumers were paid by the target company to line up! This story always reminds me of how easy it is to get tricked during a due diligence process.

Due to the difficulties in successfully achieving M&As, bear in mind that any firm or individual able to build an expertise in this is well-positioned for significant business success. At the same time, any big-scale M&A should be looked at with skepticism. As Warren Hellman, an HBS graduate and co-founder of one of the top U.S. private equity firms, says, "So many mergers fail . . . there should be a presumption of failure."[5] Or as Henry Kravis, one of history's best-known leveraged buyout experts, says, "Look, don't congratulate us when we buy a company. Congratulate us when we sell it. Because any fool can overpay and buy a company."[6]

ROLL-UP

Some people describe this strategy as "acquisitions on steroids." The usual process goes like this: An investment group purchases a number of independent companies or businesses in the same market and consolidates them into a single, new corporation.

Roll-up is a powerful strategy for some industries, and many people have made a lot of money out of it. Some of the earliest roll-ups were funeral homes and trash companies in the United States and Canada in the 1970s. Hundreds of mom-and-pop companies were "rolled up" and the mother companies became famous growth stocks. Both companies grew explosively until problems hit in the 1990s: lower-than-expected death rates coupled with increased use of cremation in the former case, and financial and operational issues in the latter. Despite their recent problems, it is important to note that the roll-up concept worked for these companies—their stock flourished for almost 20 years before the downturn.

But to be successful, a number of conditions have to be in place:

- A mature, sleepy industry without a strong dominant player and unlikely to see major new, aggressive players.
- Opportunity for significant economies of scale in key areas such as purchasing, administration, finance and accounting, human resources, branding, and marketing.
- Opportunity to improve differentiation through applying best practices in sales and marketing, or through offering customers access to wider geographic coverage, broader product line, or other benefits.
- Strong management team in place in the organization doing the roll-up, with industry and finance background to execute.

READY, FIRE, AIM

This strategy has become more popular since the beginning of the Internet Age. It is usually applied to new markets where customer behavior and demand are impossible to predict. As a result, instead of detailed strategic planning and complete product development aimed at introducing products believed to be winners, the strategy is to introduce many new products fast, hoping that one or more of them will eventually succeed. A high failure rate is accepted as a prerequisite to enable the identification of the winning products. Many observers believe that this has been the strategy of Google as it tried to develop major revenue generators beyond its search engine:

> Company officials concede that some of the newer products haven't caught on. But they say a high failure rate is baked into their strategy—as it is for an increasing number of innovative companies. Marissa Mayer, vice-president for search products and user experience, estimates that up to 60% to 80% of Google's products may eventually crash and burn. But the idea, she says, is to encourage risk-taking and let surviving products truly thrive. "We anticipate that we're going to throw out a lot of products," says Mayer. "But (people) will remember the ones that really matter and the ones that have a lot of user potential."[7]

EARLY MOVER

Sometimes a significant advantage can be gained by being the first, or one of the earliest, significant players to enter a new market. This is because an early mover can develop experience, economies of scale, and brand equity that make it difficult for competitors to catch up. Key examples are players in the Internet like eBay, Amazon, and Google. Take eBay, for example. By being an early mover in on-line auctions, it has developed a top-of-mind brand name, a major seller and buyer base (something very important for an auction business), substantial experience in catching fraud as the fraudsters were developing their own experience, and a database of transaction and feedback history on a huge population of registered users. It will be difficult for a competitor to enter the market now.

But the early-mover strategy must be applied with care. Early entry has its risks and costs: R&D, market education, legal expenses, and many others. Also early movers cannot benefit from knowledge of the successes and mistakes the others make. For example, many companies that tried to enter China when it first opened up suffered great losses as the regulatory environment and market mechanisms (such as distribution and logistics) were very primitive. Their mistakes helped many other later entrants avoid costly errors. Another example is the well-known failure of Webvan, a U.S. Internet grocer that was backed by experienced management, powerful investors, and a successful NASDAQ listing. But it filed for bankruptcy two years after its listing. One of the key investors explained the failure: "Instead of really testing the concept in one city and really perfecting it in one city, they were going to be first movers and they were going to take over the world. . . . But they were overextended from day one. One day you will see some very, very good practitioners of online grocery and upscale shopping. No question about it, but it wasn't Webvan."[8]

BUNDLING

Bundling is the strategy of selling related products or services together as a single unit (a "bundle"), often but not always at a total price lower than what the products or services would come to if they were sold separately. A bundle is often easier or more profitable to sell than the component products or services, because it can increase the competitiveness and attractiveness to customers, often at very marginal cost to the seller. For example, many hotels include breakfast in their room price. Breakfast has a high value to the customer, as a hotel breakfast is often priced at US$10 or more. But it is of very little marginal cost to the hotel.

At the same time a bundle makes life easier for customers—sometimes so much easier that customers will choose inferior products. A key example is software and media content bundling. Research by Professor Yannis Bakos of Leonard N. Stern School of Business at New York University and Professor Erik Brynjolfsson of Sloan School of Management shows that "bundling is very effective for digital 'information goods' with close to zero marginal cost (such as software, video, and news) and could enable a bundler with an inferior collection of products to drive even superior quality goods out of the marketplace."[9]

Notes

1. These strategies can all fit into Professor Porter's generic strategies. For example, Southwest Airlines is mainly a cost focus and razor-and-blade is also a low-cost strategy.
2. Dominque Fortier and Steve Foerster, "A Note on Mergers and Acquisitions and Valuations," Ivey Management Services (Canada) (2000): 6.
3. Ibid.,
4. David Harding, Sam Rovit, and Alistair Corbett, *Avoid Merger Meltdown: Lessons from Mergers and Acquisitions Leaders*, (Boston: Harvard Business Press), September 15 2004; available online: www.harvardbusiness.org (access date: February 3, 2009).

5. Terence P. Pare, "The New Merger Boom," Fortune (28 November 1994): 96.
6. Curt Schleier, *How to think Like the World's Greatest Masters of M&A* (New York: McGraw-Hill, 2001).
7. Ben Elgin, "So Much Fanfare, So Few Hits," *Business Week* (10 July 2006).
8. Sydney Finkelstein, *Why Smart Executives Fail* (New York: Portfolio, 2002), 40.
9. Yannis Bakos and Erik Brynjolfsson, "Bundling Information Goods: Pricing, Profits and Efficiency," April 1998; available online: www.ssrn.com/abstract= 11488 (access date: February 3, 2009).

15

FINAL WORDS

ONLY THE PARANOID SURVIVE

Before finishing this book, I thought it would be good to share with you some quotes that I have heard many times during my HBS days, quotes I have found extremely inspiring and practical for my personal life and consulting, investment, and entrepreneurial careers.

In the beginning of his book, *Only the Paranoid Survive*, Andy Grove, a Stanford professor and the CEO who led Intel to become the world's largest chip maker, explains what he was paranoid about when he ran Intel:

> I worry about products getting screwed up, and I worry about products being introduced prematurely. I worry about factories not performing well. . . . I worry about hiring the right people, and I worry about morale slacking off. . . . I worry about other people figuring out how to do what we do better or cheaper . . . (and) about strategic inflection points (meaning the point when business fundamentals change.)

The concept behind only the paranoid surviving is similar to what I discussed earlier in the context of Murphy's Law and the need for Plan B. However, it is more than just having a Plan B.

Getting It Right

Being paranoid in a way that promotes survival means getting Plan A right in the first place. Some examples:

- A few years ago, shortly before the announcement of a tax increase on new car purchases, the secretary of finance of Hong Kong bought a car just in time to avoid the tax increase. An employee of the car dealer tipped off the local media and a scandal resulted. Eventually, the secretary was forced to resign. The secretary had been a banker and was reasonably wealthy. So, even though it would save tax money to buy a car when he did, he *had* the money, and he would not have risked the purchase had he been more paranoid about public scandals.
- In his book, Andy Grove wrote about a major crisis at Intel around 1994, which you may well have heard of. The company was aware of a bug in its new flagship product, the Pentium processor chip. But analysis showed that an average spreadsheet user would only run into this bug once every 27,000 years. This was much longer than the time it would take for other problems common with semiconductors to crop up. So the company decided to introduce the Pentium chip despite the bug, while looking for ways to correct the defect. Unfortunately the bug was discovered by a mathematics professor and then widely discussed on the Internet. Eventually it got the attention of the mass media including CNN and major newspapers. This resulted not only in a scandal but also a write-off of almost half a billion dollars for damage control, including replacing chips for consumers who would never have run into problems with the bug itself. Again, if Intel had been more paranoid about possible consequences of the bug, it might have adopted a more cautious strategy in the first place.

Managing Change

Exercising survival-promoting paranoia also means being an expert in change management. Change is not easy. I have done a handful of process-re-engineering and change management projects in my career. Through these projects, I have come to appreciate that change is easier said than done. These are some of the barriers I have seen:

- Lack of pull from within the group that will need to change. Many people naturally resist change. Possible reasons include pressure on them to achieve short-term targets, lack of ability to see the big picture or lack of analytical skills to understand the change, reluctance to admit existing practice is out-of-date, fear of higher transparency and hence tighter control from superiors, reluctance to give up power or learn new skills, or simple inertia.
- Lack of push from the right authorities. Sometimes senior management fails to issue enough top-down pressure to drive change. This could be because management is not sufficiently determined or its power base is too weak to drive change.
- Lack of skills, tools, or resources to make the change. Sometimes people want to change but are not enabled or empowered. An example is a family company trying to implement the Balanced Scorecard. Although there seemed to be enough pull and push within the company for the change, there were simply not enough human resources for the project. The project needed technical expertise in Balanced Scorecard, analysis, project management, and other areas that the company did not have and could not afford to hire.

It is advisable to hold on to this motto regardless of your level in an organization. Being a paranoid CEO will keep you on high alert for external market and internal organizational developments. To get timely and accurate information, you will actively listen to people at all levels inside and outside your company, especially the lower-level employees who have direct contact with customers, products, and key processes. Because you are impatient of deadwood staff members that stand in the way of change, you will create a culture, an organization, and a power base conducive to change. You will actively manage any change initiative to ensure tools, training, and resources are appropriate. (See Appendix D for a leading change management tool.)

The motto is also very powerful if you are in middle management. In every reengineering and change management project I have done, there was always some dead wood. Deadwood staff members tend to be middle-aged middle management people who have been somewhat successful in the past but fail to change as market and competition demand changes in their skills, tools, and approach. This is often due to the reasons for avoiding change I described earlier. Being dead wood puts you in a very weak position. Either you eventually become obsolete or your company, because of the failure to change, becomes obsolete. Believing that "only the paranoid survive" will keep you from becoming dead wood. This is reinforced by another of my favorite quote, this one from General Eric Shinseki, retired chief of staff of the U.S. Army, who says, "If you don't like change, you are going to like irrelevance even less."

If you are only an entry-level staff member, this motto encourages you to have an inquisitive mind. Keep your eyes open for any inefficiencies, ineffectiveness, market changes, or new technologies that indicate change is necessary. Minor improvements you make can get you noticed by middle management. Major discoveries could get you a career break. The story of the Post-it Note is an inspiring one. The technology behind the low-tack reusable pressure-sensitive adhesive was invented by Dr. Spencer Silver at 3M in 1968. But for five years, Silver promoted his invention through many channels, including seminars within the company, with no success. In 1974, Art Fry, a 3M employee who had attended one of Silver's seminars, noticed a possible use for the technology: sticking bookmarks onto his hymnal for church choir. Art Fry subsequently led the development of Post-it Notes. By keeping an eye out for new technologies (by attending seminars, among other things) and being constantly on the lookout for inefficiencies, Art Fry became a well-known figure, credited with making Post-it Notes available to the market.

However, especially as an entry-level associate, you must be careful before suggesting any major changes to management. You must carefully think through the changes, test the idea, collect feedback from colleagues, and be aware of the power structure, especially the higher-level dead wood within the company. If you have an entrepreneurial idea, it may be useful to keep in mind that your observations could also become major business ideas. If the pressure-sensitive adhesive had not been a company intellectual property, it would have been an exceptional entrepreneurial venture.

HAVE THE TIME OF YOUR LIFE

Warren Buffet says, "I jump out of bed and tap dance to work every day. I'm having the time of my life!"

I am often told by professors and speakers at HBS that a critical success factor in life and in business is to do something you love doing. If you are passionate about your work, you have a much better chance of success. There can be many reasons for this. First, because you love it, you are bound to know a lot about it. Second, you will love spending time and effort on it. Your passion will be a source of inexhaustible energy. Third, life is too short to be wasted on something you do not like.

As I was told this so many times and because people who told me this were all experienced and extremely successful, I do not have the slightest doubt that it is true. However, two points about this quote:

- Most of the people from whom I have heard this are entrepreneurs or top executives. They have a lot of control over what they do. They are in powerful positions, making high-impact decisions. It is easier for them to get job satisfaction than for middle managers and entry-level associates.
- I have no firsthand, real-life experience and example to share here. I've liked all my jobs. I have been an entrepreneur and have worked as an adviser to CEOs and board members. But I have yet to "tap dance to work." When I was at my tenth-year HBS reunion in 2008, I was glad to find out I was not alone. I spoke to quite a few people who are all happy with what they are doing but they told me they are not "tap dancing to work" either. I guess for people like me, there are only two possibilities—either we eventually find a career that we are passionate about or we do not find a passion in any work (though we do like our work) and will eventually decide to retire early when we have enough investment income. Therefore, do not be discouraged if you have yet to find your passion.

STICK TO IT

"Be like a postage stamp. Stick to one thing until you get there," writes Josh Billings, a 19th-century American humorist.

Here's a story I like to tell: When a new salesman asked his manager how many calls he should make to a prospect before he gives up, the manager replied, "It depends on when one of you dies." This is an exaggeration, but determination and perseverance are indeed key success factors, especially in running a business. Running a business is not easy: getting customers, managing cash flows, organizing operations, motivating staff, fulfilling orders, fighting competition, growing the bottom line, acquiring other companies, attracting investors, and so on and on. You need to be determined to succeed.

Determined people possess the stamina and courage to pursue their ambitions despite failures, criticism, ridicule, or unfavorable circumstances. Many well-known figures in history share the same trait of determination. Who do you think I'm describing in the following list?

This was a man who:

- Failed in business at age 21
- Was defeated in a legislative race at 22
- Failed again in business at 24
- Overcame the death of his sweetheart at 26
- Lost a congressional race at 34
- Lost a congressional race at 36
- Lost a senatorial race at 45
- Failed in an effort to become vice president at 47
- Lost a senatorial race at 49
- Was elected president of the United States at age 52

This man was Abraham Lincoln.

APPENDIX A

"WHY" AND "SO WHAT"

A real-life example to demonstrate the use of "why" and "so what" to create effective financial measurements and reports:

Around 2002, when the Hong Kong economy was very depressed, I worked on a study for a leading property investment company. One of its income streams is rental from its shopping malls. The company was experiencing declining income and an even faster decline in share price. This resulted in pressures from shareholders, banks, and rating agencies. The objective of the study was to investigate how to improve performance.

When I arrived at the company, the first thing I did was look at the financial data. I found that only two major reports were readily available: the monthly financial statements and the detailed lists of the rental paid by each tenant. The study went on for three months. Here is a summary of the process:

> CONSULTANT (ME): So what do these rental figures mean? Are we doing well or not well?
>
> COMPANY EXECUTIVES: We don't know since we cannot compare with market.
>
> CONSULTANT (ME): Why not?
>
> COMPANY EXECUTIVES: Like most businesses, we don't know the details of our competitors' pricing. Even though we have some market intelligence through our tenants and agents, retail is tricky. No two shops are the same. Even if two shops are around the corner from each other, the traffic and storefront can result in very different rentals.

CONSULTANT (ME): So this means we need a way to assess our rental performance. Let's talk to our friendly competitors as well as our tenants and our staff—people who know about our competitors. Let's also try to study best practice companies overseas to see how they assess their performance.

After about a month of data collection, the results confirmed that even best-practice retail landlords could not easily compare their rentals with those of their competition. But it was found that retailers assess their store success by measuring sales per square foot. Their rental affordability has a ceiling of about 10–20 percent of sales depending on their category. For example, it is about 18 percent for fashion and 15 percent for restaurants. If a retailer's actual rent as a percentage of sales is consistently above this ceiling, this means judging from the business that the retailer is conducting, the location is too low to justify the rent. If it is consistently significantly below the ceiling, this means the rent is set too low. If many retailers in the same mall have the ratio above the ceiling, it could indicate an issue with the overall management and marketing of the mall. If most have ratios below and only a few above it, this could indicate the problem lies with the retailers, not with the mall management overall.

CONSULTANT (ME): Can we generate a report with data on sales per square foot and rent as a percentage of store sales for each tenant? We should do this by retail category, as rent affordability is different for different retail categories.

COMPANY EXECUTIVES: But we don't have sales data.

CONSULTANT (ME): Why not? Why do competitors have them and we don't?

COMPANY EXECUTIVES: Leading competitors ask tenants for a base rent plus a turnover rent. Turnover rent is a percentage of sales. For example, they may ask a tenant to pay a base rent of US$2 per square foot plus one percent of each month's sales if sales exceed a certain threshold. Say the threshold is US$100,000. If sales are below US$100,000, tenants pay $2 per square foot. If above US$100,000, they pay US$2 per square foot plus one percent of the amount over US$100,000. To calculate the dollar value of this one percent, tenants have to submit monthly store sales.

CONSULTANT (ME): Why are we not charging turnover rent?

COMPANY EXECUTIVES: Because we have little negotiation power in this depressed market.

CONSULTANT (ME): So does this mean we can never get the data?

COMPANY EXECUTIVES: Well, maybe we can charge a turnover rent with a high threshold so tenants will know they probably do not have to pay turnover rent unless business is very good. This way, turnover rent is not an income for us. It is a data source.

CONSULTANT (ME): Assuming we can have the data, we can display the data on a graph and draw some conclusions (see Figure 3.8.)

COMPANY EXECUTIVES: So what do we do after we have these conclusions?

CONSULTANT (ME): We should have an action item for each tenant. For example, if a certain restaurant tenant has low sales per square foot and high rent as a percentage of sales, we know it is not doing well in business. We should meet with its owners to discuss the problems and solutions. We should also be monitoring them very closely as small restaurant and small business owners often default on rental.

COMPANY EXECUTIVES: Yes! We once had a steakhouse owner who just closed down overnight and left town! Maybe we should also have a monthly meeting to discuss and brainstorm on actions.

So at the end of the three-month project, we set up a new rental policy, a new report format, a regular rental meeting, and a small task force that provides advisory services to tenants with depressed businesses. The client's business steadily improved. As you can see from all this, the outcome was driven by asking "why" and "so what" on financial data available.

Appendix B

Key Interviewing
Techniques for Data
Collection

Setting up the Interview

Cold calling is probably the last resort. Things will always go more smoothly if you can arrange an interview through a contact. Your chances of success are likely to be much higher if you can say, "Peter Chan referred me to you. He said you would be the right person to give me some advice." If you and the interviewee both know this middleman well, it would be a good ice-breaker to talk about some harmless and positive topics about the middleman—things like "How long have you known Peter? He is such a good golfer!" Again, this is related to the topic of social networking discussed earlier. The bigger your network, the easier it is to get the right interviewees.

Receptionists, secretaries, and personal assistants are some of the most powerful people when it comes to arranging for an interview. Show these gatekeepers that you respect them and appreciate their help. If they like you, they can always "put you through over the phone" and "sneak you into" their boss's busy schedule. If they are in a lousy mood, they can say, "Please leave your name and telephone number and I will call you if we are interested." I have a rule—at the end of my first conversation with strangers that I might need to contact again, I always ask for their name. Then I always address them by name before I hang up. I will say, "Thank you, Susie" or "I appreciate it very much, Tom." Then I will make a note of the name. I will look for the same person next time I call. I will start chitchatting a little more to get to know the person, saying, "How was your weekend?" or "It must be a busy time for you!" Some will eventually feel they are my friends and should help me. Of course, I am not saying this works every time. Nonetheless, my chances of success are higher than they'd be if I were to snub people so well-placed stand in my way.

PREPARING FOR THE INTERVIEW

Always have a list of questions to prompt you during the interview. If you do not have a list, the risks are significant. First, you may digress and fail to discuss key issues before your interview time is up. Second, you may lose your train of thought and run into "dead air" when you cannot get the conversation going. This will make you look ill-prepared and not as competent as you actually are. Designing the list is an art. The question list should be roughly in the order you would ask the questions. The order and flow should be somewhat logical so you do not seem to jump from one topic to another. More important questions should be asked earlier in case you run out of time before the end of the list. However, questions that are important but may be more sensitive (such as financials, market share, and the like) should be left to near the end of your allotted time. Hopefully by the end of the interview, the interviewee will have loosened up enough to answer such questions. If someone refuses to answer, at least leaving these questions to the end hasn't jeopardized your chances of getting the other questions answered. Each question on the list should be worded succinctly so you will not have to spend a lot of time reading it during the interview.

Some interviewees may ask you to send them the list of questions before the interview. In this case, fine-tune the list to make sure the questions are clearly and appropriately worded for the interviewee. And take out any sensitive questions. You can still try to ask them at the interview, especially toward the end of the interview. But it's better not to send them beforehand to avoid any unnecessary hiccups or alarm.

CONDUCTING THE INTERVIEW

Take notes during the interview. When I first started to do interviews, I would take very scanty notes. I was confident of my memory. I thought it would be better to focus on giving the interviewee eye contact and on listening. But I quickly found out that good interview notes are critical to ensure no details are forgotten. It is better to be safe and have the notes than to risk missing key information or appearing unprofessional when you have to call the interviewee back to get the information again.

Go deep. Although you have the list of interview questions to use as a reference, for critical areas, you should pursue the interviewee's answers and dig as deep as possible by asking why. The rule of thumb is it takes five "whys" to get to the root causes and the most fundamental issues. For example:

INTERVIEWEE: I believe this industry is declining rapidly.
INTERVIEWER: Why is that?
INTERVIEWEE: Because customers are all migrating overseas.
INTERVIEWER: What is making them migrate?
INTERVIEWEE: Because of the lower labor cost.
INTERVIEWER: Why is lower labor cost important? Why not automate?
INTERVIEWEE: Labor is over 60 percent of the cost. Automation does not work as it takes a lot of money. . . .

If the interviewee cannot answer some of your questions, you can consider asking for suggestions about sources or other interviewees if you feel the conversation is comfortable enough for that. It is especially useful if the interviewee can introduce you or can be named as your reference when you try to set up a conversation with other people who may have the answer.

After the Interview

Read and organize your notes as soon as possible after the meeting. Sometimes you will use shorthand during the interview as you try to take notes very quickly. It is much easier to remember your shorthand shortly after the interview than days later.

Think through the implications of the information as you organize your notes and update the hypothesis (discussed in Chapter 13) and list of questions.

Mail or e-mail a thank-you card or note after every interview. The card or note should be personalized, preferably recalling one or two key points you learned during the interview. This will make your interviewees feel that you have listened to them, value the time they spent with you, and see them as long-term associates rather than one-time data sources.

APPENDIX C

CAGR SHORTCUT

The following table provides a comparison of the exact CAGR as calculated by the detailed formula and the rough CAGR as estimated the shortcut Rule of 75%.

(A) Number of Years to Double (FV/PV)	(B) CAGR Calculated by Formula	C = 75%/A CAGR Calculated by Rule of 75%
2	41%	38%
3	26%	25%
4	19%	19%
5	15%	15%
6	12%	13%
7	10%	11%
8	9%	9%
9	8%	8%
10	7%	8%
11	7%	7%
12	6%	6%
13	5%	6%
14	5%	5%
15	5%	5%
16	4%	5%
17	4%	4%

(Continued)

(Continued)

(A) Number of Years to Double (FV/PV)	(B) CAGR Calculated by Formula	C = 75%/A CAGR Calculated by Rule of 75%
18	4%	4%
19	4%	4%
20	4%	4%
21	3%	4%
22	3%	3%
23	3%	3%
24	3%	3%
25	3%	3%

APPENDIX D

CHANGE MANAGEMENT
TOOL: DICE

My two mentors at BCG, Harold L. Sirkin and Perry Keenan, are very active in the field of change management. In October 2005, they, together with Alan Jackson, another vice president at BCG, published in *Harvard Business Review* a new framework, known as DICE, that delineates the four critical elements of a successful change project.[1] This framework was tested on more than 1,000 change projects and has been found to be very effective. The tool is quite consistent with my experience in change projects. I find it a useful way to try to assess whether a change project is set up for success or failure.

According to DICE, these are the four critical elements to drive a successful change project:

D: Short *duration* between reviews of the project. Reviews are generated when project teams report concrete progress toward the goal of the project. The authors suggest that complex projects should be reviewed every two weeks. More familiar projects should be reviewed every six to eight weeks, but not longer than eight weeks because "the probability that change initiatives will run into trouble rises exponentially when the time between reviews exceeds eight weeks."

I: *Integrity* of the team. This means that the project team is selected so they can be relied on for the project. The team has among its members all the necessary skills, knowledge, viewpoints, and informal power to complete the work necessary in the project. The work usually includes information collection, analysis to solve problems, project management, presentations, communications, and many other steps. The team members should also be motivated and energetic since change projects can be high pressure.

C: *Commitment* of the most powerful executives (counting both formal and informal power) as well as the key staff affected by the changes. The commitment must also be consistently communicated loud and clear to the organization: "A rule of thumb: when you (top level executives) feel that you are talking up a change initiative at least three times more than you need to, your managers will feel that you are backing the transformation."

E: Limited additional *effort* required of employees to make the change. A change project has higher likelihood of success if the effort needed for those affected to change over to the new process is limited: "Ideally, no one's workload should increase more than 10 percent. Go beyond that, and the initiative will probably run into trouble." This means that the implementation of and changeover to the new process must be carefully planned, including steps such as scheduling the change to happen during low season, hiring temporary staff, and so on, so that employees are not overworked.

Note

1. Harold J. Sirkin, Perry Keenan, and Alan Jackson, "The Hard Side of Change Management," *Harvard Business Review* (October 2005): 109–118. Quoted passages are from pp. 2, 4, and 6 of the reprint.

INDEX

A

area chart, 48, 55–59
assumption, 9, 67, 80, 82, 83, 165, 184

B

balanced scorecard, 146, 147, 164, 171–174, 213
ballpark, 183, 186, 187, 189, 192, 194
Best Alternative to a Negotiated Agreement (BATNA), 28–32, 34
big picture, 76, 77, 161, 200–201, 213
bottleneck, 89, 90, 93, 95, 97
bundling, 209

C

capacity, 89, 90, 93, 182
cascading chart, 48, 55, 56
cash, 7–18, 22, 49, 51, 149–151, 157
Compound Annual Growth Rate (CAGR), 183–187, 189, 225, 226
compounding, 7, 19, 185
connectors, 68–70, 73
consistency, 188–190
cycle time, 90

D

deductive, 39, 40, 48, 165, 183, 184, 198
DICE, 227–228
dollar cost averaging, 22, 23

E

early mover, 208–209
expenses, 8, 9, 12, 13, 16, 18, 103, 135, 151, 208

F

feedback, 94, 103, 106, 107, 114, 146, 200, 208, 214
Four P's, 119–120, 141
framing, 33

G

golden bridge, 25, 35, 36
Granovetter, 65, 67
growth-share matrix, 48–50

H

Harvey Mackay, 65, 69, 70, 71, 103
hypothesis, 175, 177, 178, 192, 193, 195–199, 200, 223

I

inductive, 39, 40, 61, 198
investment income, 4, 6, 7, 9, 10, 12, 13, 18, 215
investments, 3, 4, 6–13, 15–20, 22, 30, 32, 41, 49, 52, 66, 69, 78, 91, 112, 123, 132, 135, 142, 152, 153, 156, 157, 166, 180, 181, 188, 207, 211, 215, 217

J
Jack Welch, 102, 104
Jim Collins, 101, 103, 104

L
Law of accuracy, 191–192
Law of reciprocity, 72, 112
leverage, 8, 10, 11, 13, 17, 28, 111, 207
linear income, 3, 4, 107
logic, 16, 38, 39, 40, 41, 46, 47, 48, 61,
    62, 83, 143, 154, 165, 175–177, 184,
    197, 198, 200
loss leader, 204
low-hanging fruit, 79–80

M
mergers and acquisitions, 205–207
monopoly window, 129–132
moon chart, 48, 53–55, 125
Murphy's Law, 81, 211

N
negotiation, 17, 25–28, 30–36, 48, 70, 72,
    91, 112, 132, 157, 218
network, 65–73, 221

O
office politics, 5, 6, 108, 116

P
perspective, 6, 28, 78, 110, 120, 131, 141,
    142–144, 174, 192, 194
place, 3, 8, 28, 33, 42, 52, 72, 96, 104,
    109, 113, 119, 136–139, 151, 153,
    207, 212
Plan A, 80, 81, 212
Plan B, 80–82, 211
Porter five forces, 164, 165–169, 182
Porter generic strategies, 164,
    169–171
Porter value chain, 164, 169–171
power, 7, 28, 29, 33, 69, 70, 72, 91, 110–117,
    166, 167, 206, 213, 214
PowerPoint slides, 46, 53, 57, 177
price, 4, 5, 7, 8, 12–22, 28, 81, 119, 121–133,
    135, 151, 152, 156, 157, 203, 204, 209, 217
prioritize, 50, 75–80

process, 87–99, 107, 124, 126, 134, 141,
    144–147, 156, 157, 165, 175, 182, 196,
    197, 199, 200, 206, 207, 217, 228
process mapping, 88, 93–99
product, 46, 53, 91, 116, 119, 120, 121, 123,
    126, 128–130, 132, 134, 138, 143, 167, 180,
    182, 203, 204, 207, 208, 212
promotion, 45, 71, 119, 124,
    129–135

R
razor and blade, 203–204
ready, fire, aim, 207–208
real estate, 8–10, 12, 14–17, 81, 101, 116, 142,
    151, 190
reciprocity, 70, 72, 111, 112
reframing, 33
reputation, 109, 111, 115–117
risk, 4, 5, 9–13, 15, 17–19, 21, 22, 28, 52, 61,
    62, 82, 92, 96, 120, 122, 129, 152, 157, 169,
    179, 208, 222, 223
roll-up, 207

S
scenarios, 179, 183, 187, 188
segmentation, 121–127, 130
sensitivity, 83, 183, 186, 190
setting expectations, 76, 77
Southwest Airlines, 109, 204–205
speculation, 9, 15
stock index funds, 19
stock market, 9, 10, 17–21, 24, 101
stock options, 4, 5, 7, 104
story, 5, 10, 20, 26, 27, 31, 33, 38,
    41–43, 45, 57, 62, 71, 81, 82,
    107, 195, 197, 200, 206
storytelling, 38, 41–44, 46, 197, 199
strength of weak ties, 67
sunk cost, 151–153

T
The Tree, 164, 174–176, 198, 199
triangulation, 186, 188–190
two-by-two matrix, 48–53

W
Warren Buffett, 17–20, 200, 206